WISCONSIN'S GERMAN ELEMENT

J. H. A. Lacher's Introductory History

I0221736

Edited by
Don Heinrich Tolzmann

CLEARFIELD

Originally published by
J. H. Lacher, 1925

Additional material by
Don Heinrich Tolzmann
Copyright © 1999
All Rights Reserved.

Printed for
Clearfield Company, Inc. by
Genealogical Publishing Co., Inc.
Baltimore, Maryland
1999

Reprinted for
Clearfield Company, Inc. by
Genealogical Publishing Co., Inc.
Baltimore, Maryland
2001

International Standard Book Number: 0-8063-4909-3

Made in the United States of America

Table of Contents

iv

Editor's Introduction

This volume represents a brief introduction to the German element of Wisconsin, which was written by J. H. A. Lacher, who was a vice-president and curator of the State Historical Society of Wisconsin, and published in 1925 in Milwaukee by the Muehlenberg Unit of the Steuben Society of America. Although completed more than seven decades ago, it nonetheless provides a convenient compendium of information on the topic up to the date of its first publication. Moreover, it provides a number of valuable insights to the German-American experience, many of which are in need of further exploration and study. For these reasons, I decided to edit this work for re-publication. Those interested in other and more recent works on various aspects of the topics covered in this volume are referred to a selective bibliography listed at the end of the volume.

In the recent past, I have edited a number of works, such as this, for the sole purpose of illuminating German-American history at the state and local level and in the hopes of encouraging further research and study on the topic. This also reflects the increased interest for works dealing with German-Americana, and it is hoped that this work will address that particular interest in the case of those interested in an introduction to the topic of Wisconsin's German element.

The German element, it should be noted, is defined as including the immigrants and their offspring from Germany, Austria, Switzerland, and other German-speaking areas of Europe. In Wisconsin, the German element today comprises more than 55% of the state's population, thereby making it one of the "Germanest" states in the Union. Certainly, on statistical grounds alone, this element is worthy of not only appreciation, but of further study, and perhaps some of the dimensions illuminated here may offer the points of departure for such future work.

Finally, special thanks to Dorothy Young, Department of Germanic Languages and Literatures, University of Cincinnati, for the preparation of the manuscript.

Don Heinrich Tolzmann
University of Cincinnati

I. The German Element

1. The German Element in Wisconsin

Every individual contributes something toward the making of a community, hence, whatever we are and have accomplished as a commonwealth, is due to our situation and the various nationalities that have fused to form our population. Much has been written about the French regime, romantic indeed but of no lasting influence; of the lead region, with its western and southern frontiersmen, its Cornish and Irish; far more has been recorded about the activities of the irrepressible Yankee element with its enterprise, optimism and dominating spirit; less, much less, is known of the other ethnic units, the English, Scotch, Welsh, Irish, Scandinavian, Bohemians, Poles, Hollanders and Germans. All these elements have helped to make Wisconsin one of the most substantial and enlightened states in the Union. Somewhat familiar with the contributions of each, it would be a pleasure to give due credit to them all; but my subject being "The German Element in Wisconsin," I must perforce confine myself to my theme.

Before proceeding, I must define what is a German. For centuries Germany was merely a geographical conception, which included numerous independent states and free cities, each with its own government, coinage, tariff, army and policy. As an illustration of these chaotic conditions it may be mentioned that the territory known as Rhenish-Bavaria (a part of the old Lower Palatinate) was divided before the French Revolution into thirty-seven independent principalities, each with its own extravagant, oppressive court, patterned after that of Versailles. The people, while German, possessed no centralized nationalized consciousness, but considered their own particular principality, their dialect, and themselves superior to the others, whom they often disliked, disdained and fought. The vicissitudes of war wrought frequent changes in boundaries, including conquests by France, Russia, and Sweden, and attempted absorption by Denmark; while the state of Hanover was governed for 152 years by the royal house of England. Napoleon's conquest of Germany and his creation of larger puppet states wiped out hundreds of these petty principalities, which were not restored after the great Corsican's downfall. Yet enough remained to warrant Heine's withering sarcasm:

"And when I on St. Gotthard stood,
I heard all Germany snoring;
It slept down there in gentle care
Of six and thirty monarchs."

Although they were long under foreign rule, we yet speak of the Irish, Welsh, Norwegians and Poles. Why apply a different rule to the Germans? Have the missions of Germans recently allocated to ten different nations suddenly lost their ancient identity? The German Empire, established in 1871, did not embrace all of the old German states; therefore, following Edward Freeman, Ruskin, Carlyle, Henni, and other eminent authorities, I shall include the German Swiss, the German districts of recent Austria-Hungary, the Luxemburgers, the Germans of the Baltic provinces and of Alsace-Lorraine. (Even in France the people of the last-named province, the home of my ancestry, were long known officially as "subjects allemande du Roi France" - (German subjects of the king of France).

The Germans who settled in this country in such large numbers, whether during the colonial period, or since, came over on general or personal solicitation. Land without workers is of little value, therefore, the proprietors, patrons, grantees and speculators who had somehow acquired title to large, undeveloped tracts, have always sought settlers for their possessions through agents, advertisements and alluring promises. We know that even English prisons were ransacked to furnish colonists. Germany, often torn by religious and political dissensions, and ravaged by France, offered a promising field for their operations and, as a consequence, many thousands of Germans were settled in North America during the colonial period, while millions more have followed since the achievement of our independence. During the past century, especially, was there intense organized rivalry among the different states, and railroads with land grants, to secure settlers. In 1871, the land grants to our railroads equaled an area five times that of Pennsylvania; and all of these corporations sought settlers for their unoccupied lands so as to yield them both cash and traffic. It is true, the hope of bettering their condition - material, political and spiritual - made the immigrants responsive to the allurements of land and shipping agents.

In view of the fact that many of the pioneers of Wisconsin were descendants of the older German immigration to America, notably that to

New York and Pennsylvania, a brief notice of these is germane. Although there were Germans in the earliest settlements of the English, Dutch and Swedes, they did not arrive in great numbers until late in the seventeenth century and the beginning of the eighteenth. A large colony of Palatines (Pfaelzer) were settled by the British government in Columbia and Ulster counties, New York, in 1710, for the express purpose of making naval stores and guarding the frontier. Dissatisfied with their treatment by Patroon Livingston, who had the lucrative contract of provisioning them, most of them settled a few years later in the Schoharie and Mohawk valleys, then the remotest frontier, where they multiplied rapidly by natural increase and accessions from abroad, converting the wilderness into one of the most productive farming districts in colonial America. They suffered terribly during the French and Indian War and during the Revolution from savage raids and the bloody battle of Oriskany where they repelled St. Leger with his Tories and Indians.

Influenced by the agents of William Penn and his liberal religious charter, beginning with 1683, Pennsylvania attracted such a flood of German immigrants that as early as 1717 legislation was proposed to curb them, and accordingly law was passed in 1727 obliging every male foreigner above age of sixteen to take the oath of allegiance to the king of England. However, this did not check their coming, for by 1755 it was estimated that nearly one-half the population of Pennsylvania was of German stock. From Pennsylvania they or their descendants migrated to New Jersey, Maryland, Virginia, the Carolinas, Canada and the West, usually abreast of and sometimes ahead of the Scotch-Irish. Distinctive German settlements from abroad were also established in Virginia as early as 1714, North Carolina in 1710, South Carolina in 1732, Georgia in 1734, and Maine in 1739. Many Germans were also colonized in Louisiana in 1719-21 by John Law's "La Compagnie des Indes" for the development of that then infant French colony. Since it has been alleged in state and country histories that the Germans were never pioneers, it is pertinent to cite that highest authority on the subject, Professor Frederick Turner, who says on page 102 of *The Frontier in American History*, that in 1750 "a zone of almost continuous German settlements had been established, running from the head of the Mohawk in New York to Savannah, Georgia."

Descendants of these German frontiersmen found their way in goodly numbers to early Wisconsin, some of them men of influence. One of these was Judge John P. Arndt, a native of Pennsylvania, who located at Green Bay in 1824. A most enterprising, energetic and persevering man, he left his impress on his adopted state. He conducted the first licensed tavern and operated the first licensed ferry in Wisconsin; built the first Durham boats, which revolutionized transportation on our rivers before the application of steam power; built the first decked scow-boats, the first schooner, and the first saw mill west of Lake Michigan, and also established the first brickyard. He aided in promoting many enterprises, such as the construction of the Fox River Canal, and he served in the first territorial legislature and during subsequent terms, besides holding other important offices. He was also one of the organizers of the first temperance society west of Lake Michigan. His son, Hon. C. C. P. Arndt, then a promising attorney, was killed in Madison, in 1842, while a member of the territorial council. The census report of 1836 shows that there were seven other families of this sturdy stock at Green Bay, J. P. Arndt being credited with a family of seventy-six, which number, however, included his employees, as was then the custom.

Careful research has disclosed quite a number of representatives of this stock in preterritorial southwestern Wisconsin, mainly people who had come up the river from Missouri, Kentucky, southern Illinois and Tennessee. They brought with them their long rifles, which had proved so effective in winning the West. In speaking of his participation in the battle of Pecatonica (1832), John Messersmith, Jr., begins: "I fired my yager." The "yager" (meaning hunter), pronounced "yawger" by western pioneers who carried it even beyond the Rockies, was a German gun perfected by the Pennsylvania-German gunsmiths of Lancaster county until it greatly surpassed in range European rifles of that period, and proved to be a wonderfully effective weapon in the hands of frontier marksmen in our wars against the French, English and Indians. Making due allowance for the census taker of Crawford county in 1836, whose command of English was faulty, his spelling of German and French names were mere phonetic guesses.

However, one can decipher these heads of Palatine families: Andrick, Beaver, Cagill, Messersmith, Mires, Schultz, Shuck, Smeltser, Snyder, Stineover, Stout, Swarts, Wister, and Westrope. Among the early settlers of

Lafayette County occur these Palatine names: Bluhanz, Bleebaugh, Bush, Carish, Coons, Dering, Funk, Holtshouer, Hoover, Kindle, Hambright, Hartsough, Heindel, Helm, Hogles, Hoffman, Lutter, Mach, Olmstead, Roblin, Shellenberger, Slothouer, Stover, Welty and Zeigle. Green and other counties had likewise their share. Bishop Jackson Kemper, first Episcopal missionary bishop of the Northwest, who visited Wisconsin as early as 1834 and who subsequently became one of the most influential churchmen of the state, was of Palatine stock, his paternal grandfather being a German officer who settled with his family in Dutchess County, N.Y., in 1741. His mother was of Holland stock, all of which may have accounted not only for his foreign accent, but also for his untiring labor in the vineyard of the Lord. Kemper Hall, Kenosha, is named for him. Colonel Michael Frank, earliest abolitionist editor of the state and the father of the public free school system of Wisconsin, was a native of New York, the son of a German who fought for the American cause in the Revolution, and a Palatine mother of the Mohawk Valley. He was also one of the state's earliest advocates of temperance.

Although John Jacob Astor never lived in Wisconsin, this native of Waldorf, near Heidelberg, Germany, exercised a far-reaching influence upon the development of our commonwealth and the entire Northwest. His daring enterprise and executive ability organized and dominated the American Fur Company which wrested the fur trade of this region from the British, who had monopolized it until 1815, notwithstanding our title to the country. Chiefly through his political influence Fort Winnebago was established in 1828 to guard the important waterway used by the fur-traders on their journeys to and from Green Bay and Prairie du Chien. His inflexible rule to keep faith with the Indians and to pay them in thoroughly dependable goods, won their confidence and patronage. In 1835 he had his company erected a palatial hostelry at Green Bay, the first real hotel in Wisconsin. Although Astor never learned to spell correctly and spoke English with a strong German accent, he was intensely American and invested his profits in the country in whose destinies he believed. One of the beneficiaries of his vast fortune, not satisfied with his simple German ancestry, had himself traced to a French duke; but when his preposterous claim met with derisive disproof by French critics and press, he gave up his American birthright, went to England, and in due time acquired a title to nobility.

In spite of numerous errors, the census reports of 1840, 1850 and 1860 reveal the names of thousands of descendants of this older German immigration in Wisconsin. Sometimes they came in groups. Thus Adam Shultis, Esq., with his twelve grown children, who settled in Waukesha County in 1842, was the forerunner of the Lampmans, Nivers, Plattners, Pulvers, Showermans, Rockafellows, Silvernales and others, who came directly from the original seat of the Palatines in Columbia County, New York. In 1844 Frederick Nehs, whose ancestors came over in 1733, brought a colony of Pennsylvania Germans to Menomonee Falls, where he erected a mill and a church. But they are to be found everywhere. Colonel Gabe Bouck, attorney general, officer in the Civil War and congressman, and Judge E. Mann were of Schoharie Palatine stock. The names do not always betray their German descent, for apart from the very numerous errors made by the clerks of record, many had translated or anglicized their patronymics.

Thus, the Sharps of Elkhart Lake and of the Town of Vernon, Waukesha County, trace their descent to Jacob Scherpf, one of the original Palatine settlers of Columbia County, yet the present spelling approximates to the Palatine pronunciation of the name. The Moores of the Town of Plymouth, Sheboygan County, spelled their name originally Mohr; and Capt. William Young, early host and politician at Medina, was descended from the Jungs of New Jersey, who in the course of their peregrinations to New York, Walworth and Winnebago counties translated their German surname. Mrs. J. P. Arndt's ancestors were originally Zimmermanns, who early translated their name to Carpenter. The late Judge Milton Griswold told me that his maternal grandfather had changed his Mohawk-Palatine name of Koch to Coe, while another branch of the family write themselves Cough. Alexander Cook, a pioneer lawyer of Waukesha and for the longest time county attorney, was the grandson of a Palatine Koch, meaning cook, while his mother's father was a Hessian who had joined the Americans. A curious example was given me by the late Professor Merica, whose first paternal ancestor in America had dropped his German patronymic and taken "America," his descendants later dispensing with the initial A, leaving Merica. Many pioneer women, married to men of British stock, were of this strain, for example, Mrs. Charles (Driesbach) Westcott, the first white woman to settle in Shawano County.

After the Revolution the oncoming New England stock met the Palatines of New York and Pennsylvania in the newly opened lands of both states resulting sometimes in intermarriages. A study of thousands of Wisconsin biographies discloses many such ethnic mixtures among the pioneers, but mention of a few must suffice. Judge David Noggle, one of the founders, was of such mixed stock, as was S. U. Pinney, onetime judge of the Wisconsin Supreme Court. The mother of General Edward Bragg, war hero and congressman, was a Kohl;, her parents natives of Germany. The wife of A. G. Miller, appointed federal judge of Wisconsin in 1838, was the daughter of Prof. Kurz, a German Lutheran minister of Pennsylvania. Adam E. Ray, one of the strongest men of early Wisconsin, was likewise of this mixture, but predominantly Palatine.

The pioneer descendants of the Palatines, though still often speaking a corrupt German dialect in their homes, yet sometimes with a German education, were thoroughly Americanized and did not, therefore, usually fraternize with immigrants from Germany. The formation of church societies sometimes brought them together. Though removed several generations from the vine-clad hills of the Rhine, Mosel and the Main, they retained the principal characteristics of their ancestors: great physical strength, endurance, industry, thrift, obstinacy, and a sunny humor. They were a decided acquisition to the state.

The Germans call themselves Deutsch, and the dialects spoken in the highlands are known as Hoch-Deutsch, or High German; while those spoken in the lowlands of northern Germany are called Nieder or Platt-Deutsch, meaning Nether or Low German. This was well understood in Europe, therefore the English abroad and here usually characterized the immigrants from South Germany, Alsace, and Switzerland as Palatines, or High Dutch, while those from the Netherlands and northern Germany they called Low Dutch, but "Dutch" included them all. The onrush of German immigrants in the nineteenth century caused a differentiation, and in due time the term "Dutch" began to mean Hollanders or persons of Holland descent, hence the erroneous impression arose that the Mohawk, Schoharie, Pennsylvania, Catawba, and other hyphenated Dutch were people of Holland descent. To this day there are millions of persons, some of them highly educated, who do not know that there were any Germans in this country prior to 1848, and believe that anything "Dutch" is of Holland descent.

There were Germans from abroad in Wisconsin before 1836, especially in the lead region, among these being Fred Hollman, who settled there in 1827, and the cultured Rodolfs, who came in 1834. The most noted of these was Theodore, register of the land office at La Crosse and editor of *Der Nordstern*, a German paper he founded in 1856. A few Germans appeared in Milwaukee, then a mere hamlet, in 1835, and more arrived in 1836. Although lots and land for miles around had been taken up by speculators, some Germans found their way into the country, one of these being Frederick Hagelmeyer, who settled with his family in the Town of Greenfield in December of that year. He was the forerunner of the Würtembergers of that town. The first man to take up land in Washington County was a German. The third settler in the Town of Brookfield, now Waukesha county, was a German blacksmith named Stam. The first man to die in New Berlin was a German. These isolated examples are cited merely to show that the ubiquitous German was there at the beginning, although "unwept, unhonored and unsung."

The large subsequent influx of Germans was due neither to any effort on the part of one or more of the numerous German states, nor of any political colonization societies in this country. German political refugees founded an asylum in the United States as early as 1824 with the coming of Professors Follen, Beck, Lieber and others. In the east, in Ohio and Missouri, there were numbers of these, a few of whom hoped to establish somewhere in North America a German state, that should be a member of the United States, where they could enjoy ideal democracy and at the same time preserve their German culture and customs. Several conventions were held to further the project, the one at Pittsburgh, in 1838, with its forty delegates, being the high water mark of the movement. The idea was revived a dozen years later, but the impecunious promoters were again ridiculed by their countrymen and the German press here. Löher, their most ardent champion, complained bitterly in his publications that so many German immigrants, and especially their children forget the language of their Fatherland and become anglicized.

He deplored their lack of political solidarity, yet disclosed naively how they were handicapped when ignorant of the vernacular. It has yet to be shown authoritatively that any German State, large or small, ever promoted the emigration of its subjects to the United States. Indeed, research by

Professors Julius Goebel and Albert B. Faust in the archives of various German states has brought to light the fact that emigration to this country and its promotion was often forbidden and penalized. In 1847 and later the Prussian government tried to divert the stream of emigration eastward, while in 1879-1884, K. K. Kennan, European agent of the Wisconsin Central Railroad, was obligated to conduct his campaign from Basel, Switzerland, because of prohibitory legislation in Germany. He has told me how some of his literature would sometimes come back, marked "Verboten," but that he nevertheless succeeded in securing in a roundabout way some 5,000 settlers for his company's land grants in northern Wisconsin.

2. The Catholics

Aside from the causes of German immigration to Wisconsin already mentioned, there are several important factors which have not received adequate attention from historians. In 1829, while Vicar General Frederick Resé, a German, was in Europe soliciting workers and financial aid for the young diocese of Cincinnati, which then extended to Lake Superior, he secured the services of a number of zealous ecclesiastics and made so strong a plea at Vienna that a Catholic missionary society was organized among the most prominent people of the Austrian capital. This organization, known as the Leopoldine Society, supplied liberally not only funds and church paraphernalia, but its publications and wide influence encouraged emigration to the United States. The most distinguished of these missionaries to answer the call of Father Resé were Revs. John Henni, Martin Kundig and Frederick Baraga. The last-named, a scion of Austrian nobility, carried the gospel to the Indians of Michigan and northern Wisconsin, subsequently becoming the first bishop of Marquette. Others were Fathers Saenderl and Haetscher, who labored in the Green Bay district from 1832 to 1837. In 1833, when Father Resé was consecrated bishop of the new diocese of Detroit, Rev. Kundig followed him, locating permanently in Wisconsin in 1842. It was largely through his zeal that the diocese of Milwaukee was created in 1843, and in 1844 John M. Henni of Cincinnati became the first bishop. Strong, devoted churchmen were they, and through their influence numbers of Catholic clergymen from Austria, Bavaria and Switzerland, and thousands of Catholics from these and the Rhenish states, came to Wisconsin. Churches sprang up in large numbers; parochial schools, convents, monasteries, hospitals and orphan asylums were established. The presence of a German Catholic bishop in Wisconsin gave the territory wide publicity in Catholic states of Germany and attracted thousands hither.

Another factor in promoting German Catholic immigration hitherward was the Ludwig Verein, a missionary society with influential patrons, organized at Munich, Bavaria. Bishop Henni's visit to Europe several years after his elevation, and his interesting reports to these societies, gave further publicity to the attractions of Wisconsin as a land of opportunity to willing workers. Among the prominent clergymen whom he secured for his diocese were Reverends Michael Heiss and Joseph Saltzmann, who later became the first guiding spirits of St. Francis Seminary, established in 1850, which has probably supplied more priests to the Catholic church of this country than any other single institution. Through the good bishop's efforts, Mother Caroline, a Bavarian, founded the convent of Notre Dame in Milwaukee, in 1850. A most remarkable executive, Mother Caroline lived to see her institution develop into a large influential organization, the German School Sisters of Notre Dame, who have taught many thousands of children throughout the state and country. The original convent, where so many of Wisconsin's daughters, irrespective of creed, were educated, is not a normal school for nuns. Other influential German sisterhoods likewise founded convents in Wisconsin, among these being various orders of Sisters of St. Francis, whose motherhouses are located, respectively, at Milwaukee, Alverno, St. Francis and La Crosse; and the Dominicans at Racine. Pio Nono College was established near St. Francis Seminary for the education of Catholic teachers, and these being also trained to be organists, it has always boasted of capable professors of music, and the most distinguished being J. B. Singenberger, an outstanding figure of world-wide fame. An institution for deaf mutes soon followed. German Capuchins founded St. Lawrence College and Monastery at Mt. Calvary.

A unique German Catholic settlement was that at St. Nazians, in Manitowoc County. Under the guidance of their pastor, Father Oschwald, an entire parish from the Black Forest, Baden, was transplanted to the wilderness of eastern Wisconsin, where for a time they held property in common like the primitive Christians. The village has preserved its quaintness to this day. Due especially to the long dominance of the German element in its hierarchy and laity, the Catholic Church has been a powerful factor in the settlement and development of Wisconsin, and its story is deserving of a more adequate notice, but lack of space forbids a more extensive consideration of its beneficent influence. Since the beginning the metropolitan See of Milwaukee has been governed by men of this stock – Henni, Heiss, Katzer and Messmer – all eminent scholars and great executives. All but one of the bishops of La Crosse have been Germans: Heiss, Flasch and Schwebach. Four of the six bishops of Green Bay were of this element: Krautbauer, Katzer, Messmer and Fox, the last named a native of that city, but of German parentage. Such was also the first bishop of Superior, Rt. Rev. A. F. Schinner, since transferred to Spokane, Washington.

3. The Lutherans

Protestant church organizations and foreign mission societies in the German states proved likewise strong factors in the settlement of Wisconsin. In consequence of the attempt made by the Prussian government to unify the two dominant Protestant churches, many Lutherans who adhered strictly to their time-honored tenets and were not affected by modernism, migrated in the second quarter of the last century to America, pilgrims hoping to find an asylum where they might worship God according to their own convictions. Pastors came with their entire flocks. The first of these to reach Wisconsin was in 1839, when they established themselves in heavily timbered Washington County, founding Kirchhayn and Freistadt, these names signifying, respectively, "church grove," or refuge, and "free city," suggestive of the religious and civic freedom they hoped to attain. Others settled in Milwaukee, and a few years later similar settlements were made at Lebanon, Dodge County, and near Ixonia, Jefferson County. These and thousands of other Lutherans who followed them hailed largely from northern Germany, where foreign mission societies were active. Among these may be noted those at Mecklenburg, Langenberg-Elberfeld, and Berlin; but there were also influential societies at Basel, Switzerland, and near Nürnberg, Bavaria.

Modest though their beginnings, the German Lutherans of the state have developed into large influential bodies, with a story of singular interest. A number of missionaries, clergymen of university training, were sent to Wisconsin by these German societies. Among these was Rev. J. Muehlhaeuser, who arrived in Milwaukee in 1848, where he soon afterward organized Grace Church. He was a strong man and few Wisconsin Germans had a more far-reaching influence. In 1850 the Wisconsin Synod was organized, mainly through his efforts, and he became its first president. His patient persistence persuaded Rev. W. A. Passavant, the remarkable German-American Lutheran philanthropist of Pittsburgh, to found Passavant Hospital in 1863, a model institution, now known as Milwaukee Hospital, still conducted by the Protestant Deaconesses, a zealous organization of Lutheran women introduced from Germany by the sainted Passavant.

The Lutheran churches increasingly more rapidly than the number of clergymen supplied from abroad and the older American states, the establishment of a theological seminary was deemed imperative. A tour to Europe in 1863 by Rev. J. A. Bading for the purpose of raising funds proved so successful that a beginning was made that year, but the building was not completed till 1865, when Northwestern College, Watertown, was dedicated. It is noteworthy that its first president was Prof. Adam Martin, a graduate of Hamilton College, New York, and that from the start the English language was prominent in its curriculum. Scholarly men, graduates of famous German universities, subsequently served on the faculty of Northwestern, the most brilliant of these being Dr. A. Hoenecke, Dr. A. F. Ernst, Dr. F. W. A. Notz and Prof. E. E. Kowalke. Among its graduates are many noted clergymen and educators. At a later period the theological department was transferred to the new seminary at Wauwatosa, a flourishing institution under the auspices of the joint synods of Wisconsin, Minnesota, Michigan and other states. Prof. J. Koehler is now president. Concordia College, Milwaukee, supported and conducted by the Ev. Lutheran synods of Missouri, Ohio and other states, was opened in 1881, with Rev. C. F. W. Huth, D. D., as president. Primarily a preparatory theological seminary, the college curriculum includes the advanced studies of universities, besides an academic department for younger students. Among the prominent members of the faculty are Rev. M. J. F. Albrecht, president from 1893 to 1921, Rev. C. Chr. Barth, now presiding, and Prof. Carl Ross. The late Paul Reinsch, diplomat and statesman, was an alumnus of Concordia, as are numerous clergymen, educators and businessmen. This church also boasts of a boarding school and missions for the Indians in Shawano County.

The German Lutherans, with more than 500 churches and nearly as many parochial schools; form the largest single body of Protestants in the state, but yielding to destiny there are now fifteen English Lutheran churches in Milwaukee alone, while practically all of those in the city still adhering to the mother tongue hold services in both German and English. This transition is due to the fact that except in isolated communities, the young people prefer the vernacular; hence, the church bows to the inevitable, as it has done in the Carolinas, where the German language has been entirely superseded by the English in the Lutheran services. It is impossible to enumerate in a sketch of this scope all the benevolent and educational institutions of this important religious body; suffice it to say that they are a credit to the state.

4. The German Evangelical Synod of North America

In pioneer days the members of this church likewise received aid from Protestant mission societies of the German states. The aid received from abroad consisted not merely in a large number of well-trained missionaries – the Basel Mission House alone supplying eighty to this denomination in America – but also funds, books, church-paraphernalia, and even devout, cultured brides who bravely ventured across the stormy Atlantic to share the hardships, privations and intellectual isolation of some of these frontier preachers. Some of these were appointed "Reiseprediger," itinerant preachers whose arduous duty it was to search for their churchless countrymen in the new settlements, ministering often in farm houses and organizing congregations wherever circumstances warranted. The names of a few of these wayfaring preachers have been preserved, others are forgotten; but the sacred seed sown by them in the long ago has grown into an imposing tree – the flourishing District of Wisconsin, with more than 100 churches and a membership approximating 30,000 souls.

One of the most devoted pioneer preachers was Rev. Caspar Ruegg, who served Christus Church, near Rockfield, for more than fifty years. He also organized the churches at Slinger, Rockfield, and Menomonee Falls. He never accepted a salary during his entire pastorate, prepared and memorized 5,680 sermons, still preserved, and visited the sick irrespective of creed, walking sometimes ten miles for the purpose giving them spiritual comfort and often a bottle of wine. Rev. George Hirtz, long the pastor of Trinity Church, Fourth and Lee, Milwaukee, and Rev. Rudolf Rami, served in the Wisconsin District for more than sixty years. While not the earliest workers in the State, these also deserve mention: Revs. C. G. Haack, Louis von Ragué the friendly son of a Prussian cavalry captain, worked untiringly, yet happily among the struggling churches in the woods of Sheboygan county from 1864 to 1870, then for two years in and about Milwaukee. Transferred to other fields, he had, at his death in 1910, organized thirty churches. The church has likewise been aided by an organization of devoted deaconesses, represented in Milwaukee by a splendid hospital, over which Rev. Bruno Howe presides.

Here are the names of the oldest or more notable churches of the Wisconsin District, with the dates of their organization: - Christus, near Rockfield, 1843; St. Johannes, South Germantown, 1844; St. Paul's Calumet Harbor, 1847; St. Johannes, Slinger, 1848; and Friedens, near Jackson, 1852; St. Paul's Ackerville, 1853; Friedens, Port Washington, and St. Johannes, Town Herman, 1854; St. Johannes, Kohlsville, and St. Marcus, T. Mosel, 1855; Jacobi, Meeme, 1856; St. Peter's T. Rhine, 1858; St. Paul's, T. Russell, 1860; St. Marcus, Fillmore, 1861; Trinity, Milwaukee, and St. Johannes, Monroe, 1862. St. Paul's , the big church at Wausau, was organized in 1863 by Rev. H. Waldman. That year saw also the beginning of the large congregation at Ripon, and of Johannes at Cecil; while St. Paul's, T. Scott, New Bethel, Black Wolf, and St. Paul's, Menomonee Falls, were organized in 1867. Friedens, Milwaukee, and Friedens, Fond du Lac, were established in 1869; Trinity, Portage, 1870; St. Johannes, Black Creek, and St. Paul's, Silver Creek, 1871; St. Peter's, Saukville, 1872; Neenah, 1873, and St. Johannes, Hartford, 1874. English is making strong inroads on the mother tongue, especially in the cities, 3,850 German services being reported in 1923 against 1,420 in English. Rev. Henry Niefer – sympathetic, learned and eloquent – is now president of the Wisconsin District.

5. The German Reformed Church

Pastor Johannes Megapolensis, a Mecklenburger, who began his ministry in New Netherland in 1642, was the forerunner of thousands of German pastors and members who followed him to these shores. Just 200 years later the first services of the German Reformed Church in Wisconsin of which there is any record were held at the home of Christian Damm, in the Town of New Berlin, Waukesha County. However, the first church organization was that of the Swiss colony of New Glarus, in 1845, which seems most fitting because Zwingli, one of the founders of this denomination, was erstwhile a pastor in the Canton of Glarus, Switzerland. Its next foothold was among the immigrants from the little principality of Lippe-Detmold who had settled in the primeval forest of Sheboygan County, in 1847. It is a mooted question whether the Reformed Church erection in New Berlin in 1849 antedates that which the Lippers and Rhinelanders built in Manitowoc County, though the latter is usually considered third. The church at Sheboygan was dedicated in 1853, followed by that in Milwaukee. The Sheboygan Classis, or presbytery, was organized in the Town of Herman of that county in 1854, by Rev. Dr. J. Bossard, Revs. A. Winter and H. A. Muehlmeyer, and Elders Chr. Stoelting and H. Helming. The Classis became a member of the Ohio Synod.

There being a dearth of clergymen for the large, promising field, it was resolved at the annual meeting held at Lowell, Wis., in 1860, to establish a Mission House, or theological school, at Immanuel Church, town of Herman, and with generous support of the local laymen, the first seminary was completed in 1864. After passing under the control of several synods, the school prospered, new buildings being added to satisfy a larger attendance and a broader curriculum, which in time included academic, collegiate and theological classes. Among the 1,279 active clergymen of the German Reformed Church in the United States, 223 are graduates of the Mission House. Many of its alumni have become prominent not only in the church, but also in secular pursuits. The church calendar for 1921 records sixty churches in Wisconsin where only German services are held and sixteen in which both German and English are used. This church organization has likewise helped to people our state and to develop it spiritually as well as materially.

6. The Evangelical Association

The Evangelical Association is an American church, founded in Pennsylvania in 1800 by Rev. Jacob Albrecht, who though of German parentage, was a native of that state. The first clergyman of this denomination to reach Wisconsin was Rev. John Lutz, who arrived on horseback from Ohio in January, 1840, holding his initial services in the Town of Greenfield, Milwaukee County. He also preached to the German pioneers of the towns of Lake and Granville. In 1841 and 1842 the rapidly increasing number of German settlers brought visits from Revs. Adam Stroh, Chr. Linter, F. Wahl and G. A. Blank. In 1843 two log churches were erected, the first in the town of Greenfield, the other in Lake. Thereafter the tireless circuit riders of this zealful church followed the advancing German pioneers into the forests and openings of southern and eastern Wisconsin, preaching in private houses, organizing stations and building churches, suffering the greatest hardships, content with the meager salary of $50 a year and the shelter and sustenance offered by their poor, but generous followers. When Bishop Seybert made his first official visitation, he was so impressed with the prospects that he persuaded Frederick Nehs to establish in 1844 the Pennsylvania German settlement about Menomonee Falls. Among other circuit riders of the forties may be mentioned Revs. Joseph Harlacher, Levi Heisz, J. G. Miller and his brother, Jacob J. Miller, an Alsatian, who later became a bishop with an international reputation as a forceful speaker and strong executive.

Zion's Church, at the southeast corner of Fourth and Cedar, Milwaukee, was organized in 1846. In 1847 Jefferson built a church, and Racine in 1848. The first camp meeting in the state was held among the zealous Würtembergers of the town of Greenfield in 1849. In 1850 the church in the town of Brookfield was dedicated, the first church among the Swiss in Sauk County in 1851, and thereafter others followed in rapid succession. In 1853 men and women walked forty miles to attend services near Princeton. From 1855 to 1857 preaching stations were established in Monroe, Buffalo, Brown and Manitowoc counties. In 1857 the Wisconsin Conference was organized. In that year the first church in the Lomira district was dedicated, and in 1859 that at Hartford. In 1860 a mission was established among the Alsatians about Sharon, Walworth County, who demanded German services.

One of the noted clergymen of western Wisconsin of this period was Rev. Henry Esch, father of Interstate Commerce Commissioner John J. Esch. Since those pioneer days the Evangelical Association has spread all over the state, a beneficent influence in the spiritual life of its numerous followers and an important factor in attracting Germans and Americans of German descent to Wisconsin. The church has always been a strong advocate of temperance. In 1920 the Association counted ninety-three churches in the state, but in many of them German was no longer used exclusively, while in others it was discontinued altogether.

The above are the principal religious denominations among the Germans, which have also promoted immigration to Wisconsin; nevertheless, there are several smaller organizations deserving mention. Foremost among these are the Moravians, distinguished in colonial times for their zeal, culture and refinement, their successful missions among the Indians, and their usefulness on the frontier during the French and Indian War and the Revolution. They began operations with their customary zeal about Watertown and Green Bay in the early fifties. They now have a bishop, Rt. Rev. Karl Mueller, and about 4,000 members in the state, chiefly of German descent. The English speaking denominations have all been active among the Germans, the Methodists alone having six German churches in Milwaukee. However, it is only a question of time when these will be absorbed by the English speaking church.

7. The Liberals

The organizations heretofore mentioned were all conservative, but there was also another German element, whose representatives by their enthusiasm, force and daring stood for years in the forefront of their countrymen; who had not only attracted thousands of their kind from the Fatherland and the East, but likewise reacted in many ways upon the people of Wisconsin. These were the Liberals iconoclasts as to orthodoxy as well as autocracy, their views on religion ranging from deism to unbelief. They appeared here quite early, the fiery Dr. Francis Huebschmann, who came to Milwaukee in 1842, its first German physician, being the leader of these pioneers. But upon the failure of the uprising in Germany in 1848, thousands of political refugees fled their country and sought to realize their democratic ideals in the Great Republic. Wisconsin, like other states, welcomed them with open arms. Known by the date of their ill-fated revolution as "Forty-Eighters," they did not reach the state in numbers until 1849 and subsequently. They included many cultured persons who, with the various societies organized by them, left their impress upon the state.

The most influential of these were the Turners, gymnastic societies whose aim was the thorough physical and mental training of their members to fit them for better citizenship; in a word, they became schools of practical patriotism. After previous efforts, a permanent organization was effected in 1853 through the agency of August Willich, a Forty-Eighter, who later made such a fine record in the Civil War as a general from Indiana. The Turnverein Milwaukee, as the society was called, soon had companions in the city of its origin and in many places, large and small, resulting in a federation in the state and nation, winning national and international laurels, especially under George Brosius, a veteran of the Civil War, who for fifty years served as its physical director. In connection with the German-English Academy, a national normal school for teachers of gymnastics was established. Although not as strong as formerly, the Turners still pursue their useful activities.

While not confined to the liberals, the organization of singing societies was another manifestation of their social activities. Like the Turner societies, they sprang up among the liberals wherever they were in sufficient number. Soon a state federation was formed, with annual song festivals and contests, and affiliation of the larger societies with the great national federation. The liberals also organized "Freie Gemeinden," serving as social and ethical centers for the dissemination of the principles of liberalism, science and general knowledge. Such "free congregations" and the societies of "free men" spread likewise to the smaller communities of liberals in the state. The presiding officer, usually a man of superior culture, also functioned at funerals. Like some of the religious denominations, the liberals had their press, given to acrimonious controversy with their orthodox countrymen, especially Catholic, as well as to ethical, patriotic and scientific reading. Few of these societies survive, their stoical virtues generally passing with the founders into the indifferentism of the second and third generations, or the call of conventionality has led their descendants back to the church. The liberals, like their orthodox countrymen, boast of many proud names, but mention of a few must suffice: Schurz, the Salomons, Peter Engelmann, Huebschmann, Fritz and Matilda Anneke, Balatka, Christian Bach, Krez, Domschke and Richard Guenther. It was largely the liberals who won the title of "German Athens" for Milwaukee in the long ago.

The story of the "Forty-Eighters" has yet to be written. Their profound influence in the anti-slavery movement and in the Civil War has been given scant credit. Edmund James, long the distinguished president of the University of Illinois, said in 1906: "The influence of the 'Forty-Eighters' at this great critical time in our national life was, to my mind, decisive. They turned the balance of power in favor of universal liberty. And if sometimes they were obstinate and difficult material, this very defect was perhaps an outgrowth of their virtues. They might not have been the tower of strength they were for the Union cause had they not had the very defects which sometimes irritated and tired us."

8. The German Jews

The very large majority of the Jews of Europe and America speak Yiddish, an old German dialect containing an admixture of Germanized Jewish and foreign words and using Hebrew characters in its literature. This signifies that when the Jews were excluded for centuries from England and exiled from other countries, they had an asylum in Germany, which, though not a bed of roses, enabled them to maintain themselves and their religion, and caused their Germanization, they being always loyal to their adopted country. German Jews found their way to Wisconsin at an early day, some of the English Jewish traders being of German parentage. Such was J. M. Levy, a pioneer merchant and most enterprising citizen of La Crosse, locating there in 1845 with his German born wife, but he had been preceded in 1842 by Samuel Snow (Dutch Doc), a native of Germany. But wherever the German Jews were located, they usually identified themselves with the social activities of their Christian countrymen from abroad. In 1849 the first Jewish services were held in Milwaukee, and in 1858 the first synagogue was erected. There are at present Jewish temples not only in the metropolis but also at Appleton, Green Bay, La Crosse, Sheboygan and other points in the state. In Milwaukee they have an excellent hospital. They have also

22

benevolent organizations. Among the most prominent Jewish names of the pioneer period are those of Adler, Friedman, Friend, Hammel, Heineman, Hirschheimer, Landauer, Mack, Mann, Morawetz, Rice, Rosenheimer, Pereles, Silber, Stern, Weil.

II. German Influences

1. The Influence of the German Element

Although the Germans who came to Wisconsin in such large numbers were remotely related to the Anglo-Americans in blood and speech, they differed from them and the other elements of our population in language, education, customs and characteristics; hence their accession must have affected in many ways the development of the state, its institutions and people. Having for years devoted much time to the study of this interesting subject, I shall here give a brief outline of the results of my research. In every instance I can furnish authority to substantiate the statements made. The conspicuous virtues of the German immigrants were industry, thoroughness, thrift, honesty, a strong sense of duty, sociability, and a love of home and music. This does not mean that all had these admirable qualities. Thus, although their honesty gave rise to the phrase current years ago, "As honest as a Dutchman," some precious rascals could be found among them; but, on the whole, the characterization was true. While engaging chiefly in farming, many of them had not been farmers abroad, but artisans, tradesmen and professional men. The craftsman, being skilled by a long, thorough apprenticeship, could utilize his ability to advantage even on the farm; but for the others it was more difficult, owing to language and prejudice, except in German settlements.

Apropos, grouping is not peculiar to Germans, but is observed in all nationalities. Indeed, the Germans are more widely distributed over the country than any other foreign element. Thus a few members of the Evangelical Association removing from Prairie du Sac to Buffalo County in 1856, their glowing descriptions of the new country drew other brethren after them, in this manner establishing new units of that church. The aloofness of the German pioneers was only partly their fault, for the Yankee seldom liked foreigners and rarely recognized them socially unless these were rich or distinguished. A French physician, who had sojourned for a time in Milwaukee, complained bitterly to Dr. Huebschmann in 1843, of this unsocial trait of the Yankees. I shall now endeavor to show specifically but briefly the influence of the German element upon the various activities of Wisconsin.

2. Agriculture

The exhausted and abandoned farms of the Anglo-native pioneers have been excused on the ground that there was always plenty of cheap virgin soil to replace them. And that superficial, large-scale farming was, therefore, justified. This is a poor excuse for wastefulness and inefficiency, for after two centuries of cultivation by German stock, Lancaster County, Pennsylvania, still ranks as one of the most productive in the country. Although handicapped in many ways, the Germans of Wisconsin early demonstrated their superiority as farmers, such authorities as the Waukesha *Democrat*, the Watertown *Chronicle*, and the Rock County Agricultural Society seventy years ago contrasting their thoroughness and success with the superficial, slipshod methods of their Yankee neighbors. The Waukesha *Democrat* of July 23, 1850, says:

> Washington County – We had an opportunity, last week in passing through this county, observing its rapid settlement and improvement. The country is settled principally by German and Irish emigrants, on small farms, and by their industry the heavy timber is rapidly disappearing and their settlements assume the appearance of prosperity and comfort rarely witnessed in so new a country. Many of the German farms do not exceed ten to twenty acres, and the labor of clearing the land and putting it in crop is performed entirely by hand – men, women and children, all engaging in the work. We never saw better cultivation, the small fields having the appearance more of well-tilled gardens than common grain fields. The labor is performed with long, sharp hoes, made for the purpose, and with them all roots and grubs are removed; the crops are sufficient evidence of the perfect manner in which they are attended to. Washington County will, in a few years, unless the present population becomes so Americanized as to quit their small farms for larger, the perfect for the imperfect cultivation, be one of the most productive in the state.

Although modern machinery has enabled their descendants to farm on a larger scale, Washington and adjoining counties, populated by German stock, still produce excellent crops, while spacious buildings and herds of sleek cattle grazing on a thousand hills, and numerous substantial churches and schools attest progress and prosperity.

Upon my return to Wisconsin, in 1897, after living for some years in Minnesota, a Badger asked me what I thought of the former in comparison with the latter. Thinking particularly of eastern Wisconsin, won from a most forbidding wilderness by the Germans, I replied:

> When I think of the appalling work required to clear Wisconsin of its heavy timber and deposits of stone; when I see great heaps of stone and massive walls enclosing your farms, monuments to industry, and compare it all with the prairies of Minnesota, I must conclude that man made Wisconsin, but God, Minnesota.

It is claimed that when the Germans began to arrive in numbers after 1839, they were forced to settle in wooded eastern Wisconsin, because the New England stock had already acquired title to the choice prairies and openings of the southeastern part. James W. Woodworth, a pioneer of 1837, writing to the Old Settlers Club of Ozaukee County, in 1874, said:

> Quite a few Americans and Irish began to settle in 1838-1839, but part of them became sick of so much toil and hardship, and having no money left, embraced the first opportunity, when the Germans came in 1840, to sell out – for a trifle, and either left the country entirely or took new farms in other parts of the state.

One word more on this point. Commenting on the poor farming of the American pioneer, W. W. Daniels, professor of chemistry and agriculture, University of Wisconsin, said in the *History of Washington and Ozaukee Counties*, Chicago, 1881: "In the rapid settlement of the northwestern states this change has come more rapidly with the replacement of the pioneer farmers by immigrants accustomed to better methods of culture." "Masterful and wasteful," Frederick Turner calls the American pioneer. It was not merely that the German farmer was more thorough and industrious, but he also rotated his crops scientifically and fertilized his fields, also taking better care of his stock, implements, and all his belongings.

A notable contribution to the agricultural products of Wisconsin was the growing of barley and hops. The Germans introduced lager beer, a brew aged for months in cool vaults. Becoming popular among all nationalities during the Civil War, because the imposition of a heavy tax on distilled liquors had greatly increased their price, the ensuing enormous consumption of milder beverage created a demand for barley and hops, ingredients used in its production, until thousands engaged in their cultivation. The Germans introduced truck gardening, raising varieties of vegetables new to the country, which they sold at the German market. They also introduced the culture of the grape and made wine in Sauk, Sheboygan, Waukesha and Washington counties at an early date. The Swiss of New Glarus began to make their famous cheese soon after their arrival, while the Germans of

Dodge County made brick and limburger. This county also gained fame by fattening geese for the market, Watertown goose being now known the country over. The first horticultural society of the state was organized in 1845, with a number of German members, who often captured the first prizes. One of the state's most noted horticulturists was George Peter Peffer, a native of Germany, who settled in the town of Pewaukee in 1841. He developed many varieties of fruit, some of which are still popular. He had charge of Wisconsin's horticultural exhibit at the New Orleans World's Exposition in 1885. The once maligned carp, now recognized as a valuable food fish, is another German contribution, as is the German brown trout. We also owe to the same influence the introduction of the Hungarian pheasant, or German Rebhuhn, now the farmers' friend and hunters' delight in some of the southeastern counties. These contributions compare favorably with the English sparrow and Canada thistle.

Although the enterprising "masterful" Anglo-American element took the lead in organized effort to develop the dairy industry, the support of the careful, industrious, thrifty German farmers made success on a large scale possible. A general cannot achieve victories without a well disciplined army. Even in pioneer days, when the Yankee's livestock had often at best only an open shed for shelter, the German housed his farm animals in warm barns. In this connection it is well not to overlook the efficient German farm hand, and the German hired girl, generally present on the better Yankee farms, who, according to I. N. Stewart, were strong factors in their success. Sixty-five years ago the Ruble brothers of Rock County, with their fine 900 acre farm were among the leading breeders of blooded stock in the state. Julius Rust, a native of Bremen, who came with his parents to Milwaukee County in 1850, was the pioneer breeder of pure-bred Holstein cattle, the breed upon which rests the fame of Wisconsin's dairy industry.

The name itself is significant of German influence. The Swiss of Green County introduced the Swiss brown cattle, likewise good dairy stock. Needless to say that many others of German strain have been prominent breeders, among the foremost being Fred Pabst, and August Knospe of Juneau, repeatedly national first prize winners, and Adam Seitz & Sons, of Waukesha County, whose herd of Ayrshires is one of the very best in the country. H. F. Krueger has gained fame as a developer of grain. The Swarts brothers, whose German grandparents settled in Waukesha County in 1844, were the pioneers in raising alfalfa successfully in Wisconsin. Adam Grimm of Jefferson was the father of scientific beekeeping in the state. They are also among the leaders in other branches of agriculture. The late Henry Krumrey, of Plymouth, earned the gratitude of dairymen by organizing the Wisconsin Cheese Producers' Federation, a co-operative movement which marketed for its patrons 29,000,000 pounds of cheese in 1924. And lest we forget, agricultural science, taught in special schools in Germany years before its study was introduced here, received the attention of the German press in Wisconsin. These had special departments on farming and horticulture, issued annual premium books on the subject, and by 1870, there were German farm papers published with a large circulation.

Local farm societies were organized, such as the Plymouth Farmer Verein, which met once a week during the winter to discuss not only farming, but subjects ranging from the tariff to evolution. This society eventually brought about the organization of the Sheboygan County Fair, held annually at Plymouth. According to the Wisconsin *Agriculturist* of February, 1893, the later German immigrants were of the same type as the precursors. Says this authority under the caption of "Careful Farming":

> Our German residents who are engaged in the business of farming are proverbially thrifty and successful. We are led to reflect upon the reason for this recently when going through a comparatively new region that had been largely settled by them. The fields, to be sure, were clean and well cultivated but not strikingly different from others in this respect as to care for special mention; but every farm possessed a good barn. The houses were small and cheap, as a rule, and no more money had been expended on them than was required to make them serve the stern necessities of life; but the barns were large and substantial, and what is more, they were utilized. The crops were housed in them and not left exposed in the fields. There was room for all the stock, so that it could be kept clean and comfortable. We presume that these barns had been built only by the most stringent self-denial. Perhaps money had been borrowed and the farm mortgaged in order to do it. If so, it was the part of wisdom for it is just as true that a good barn will earn double the interest on its cost each year as it is true that a poor barn will make a poor farmer.

3. Art

Coming from a country where art had been cultivated for centuries under the patronage of church and state, the artistic influence of the Germans upon their new environment cannot be over-estimated, more particularly since puritanic traditions were still strong in America. The German Catholics, especially, through their affiliations abroad, secured gifts of beautiful paintings, altars, statuary, vestments, chalices, ostensoriums, etc., for their churches. Thus Father Inema, a Tyrolese, received from the king of Bavaria for the church at Roxbury a painting of the Virgin and Child by Kaulbach. As early as 1846 there was a German artist located in Milwaukee, and in 1850 came Henry Vianden, the picturesque, beloved artist who taught so many society ladies, among them Mrs. Frackelton, who became successful as a teacher in decorating ceramics. However, a number of his male students, such as Marr, Koehler, Enders, Schade and others attained greater distinction. Carl Marr, born in Milwaukee in 1858, the son of a German engraver, continued his studies in Munich, where he attained international fame as one of the greatest painters of his times.

Before the advent of moving pictures, when panoramas were the vogue, Milwaukee was an art center where these were painted for distribution throughout the country. The realistic backgrounds depicting the natural habitat of the mounted animals in the Milwaukee Museum are now the only reminders of this once flourishing profession. In the early years of statehood there were many German teachers of drawing and embroidery in Wisconsin. The art-glass and all the wood-carving produced in the state is the work of Germans. Germans have predominated in architecture, among the best being Victor Schulte, architect of St. John's Cathedral; H. C. Koch, designer of the city hall, and Alfred C. Clas, who with his associate, Ferry, designed the stately libraries at Milwaukee and Madison. Lithography, a German invention, was brought by them to Wisconsin. Landscape gardening and the public park system are chiefly indebted to the German element. Quentin's Park, Milwaukee, now Lapham's was originally a private park of great beauty.

The Germans early introduced amusement parks, among the later ones being Luedemann's on the river, and Luedemann's on the lake, now Lincoln and Lake parks, respectively. Christian Wahl, the father of public park system of Milwaukee, was a cultured German. And only recently, John A. Latsch of Winona, Minn., donated a large natural park near Trempealeau to his native state. The German theater has had a long career of success in Milwaukee, notably during the past three decades, when a stock company of artists has rendered with great excellence the leading dramas of the German, English, and French stages. Before the world war students of German in the high schools were favored with special matinees as a part of the school curriculum. Here, too, were heard some of the greatest performers on the German stage in Europe. Amateur and traveling troupes for years gave theatrical performances in the various German centers of the state. In a humbler way the German immigrant spread artistic taste. Regardless of hardships and endless work, he (or rather she) would have his flowers. Says I. N. Stewart on this point: "The early settler had many trials and many tasks. There was not time for ornamentation. It was years before thought was turned to planting trees and flowers. But the German never forgot the flower bed." Said J. K. Meidenbauer, a pioneer of New Berlin, years ago to his Yankee neighbor: "Some men are fools about horses and others about women, but I am a fool about flowers," in allusion to his propensity for buying rare flowering plants. So Wisconsin is indebted to the Germans for this and other "foolish" esthetic traits.

4. Diet

The presence of the Germans has also affected our diet favorably, for our cuisine owes to them many new dishes. Perhaps the chiefest of these is sauerkraut. Called "liberty cabbage" during the late war on account of its origin, this homely dish has come into its own, being now recognized as one of the most healthful, nourishing foods and enjoying great popularity. Cole slaw (from Kohl Salat, meaning cabbage salad), potato salad, dill pickles, sour meats, Hasenpfeffer, Hamburger steak (yclept Salisbury steak during the war), Vienna (Wiener-weenies) Frankfort, Mettwurst and other kinds of delicious sausage, goulash, Koenigsberger Klops, noodles, pickled green beans, celeriak, endive, chives, leeks, dill, spinach, asparagus, kohlrabi, red cabbage, sugar beets and many other good things to eat we owe to the German element. German bakers, who soon predominated, introduced zwieback, honey cakes, cheese cake, hard rolls, poppy rolls, crescents, schnecken, pretzels, coffee cake, stollen, pfeffernuesse, schaumtorten, marzipan, springerle, Vienna bread, rye bread with caraway seed, pumpernickel, etc., including those highly artistic wedding cakes in vogue years ago.

German housewives were usually good cooks and bakers, close students of cook books brought from Germany, whose authors were chefs of princes and prominent hotels. Their soups and stews, their German pancakes and Berliner Pfannkuchen, Apfel and Kirschkuchen, potato dumplings and pancakes, potato beer and wine soups, their waffles and many other delicious dishes of which I have partaken during a long life, still make my mouth water. The German cooks also excelled in the preparation of vegetables, an art unknown even in the best hotels forty years ago. Mrs. John P., Arndt, of Green Bay, who presided over the kitchen and table of the first licensed tavern in Wisconsin, "prepared many delicious Holland dishes," wrote a historian who, like so many, erroneously supposed that the Pennsylvania-Dutch are of Holland extraction.

Since that early day German hostelries in Wisconsin have generally enjoyed a good reputation. I cannot refrain mentioning a few landlords whose cuisine gave gustatory pleasures that still linger in my memory: Chas. F. Kletzsch, who began with the old Webster House, Newburg, in 1858, and whose sons are still interested in the Republican Hotel, Milwaukee, which under his management enjoyed a national reputation; Albert Scherer, Fountain City, whose delicious game and fish dinners at fifty cents were unsurpassed forty years ago; genial Charlie Hufschmidt, who closed his long career as landlord of the Dousman House, Prairie du Chien, in 1908; Fred Bertram, under whose regime the Beaumont, Green Bay, was unsurpassed in the Northwest; and Louis Ballschmieder, of Sheboygan Falls, whose meals were a revelation to his guests. And we must not forget the St. Charles, Milwaukee, for years the leading German hotel under the management, respectively, of Wettstein, Upmann and Fernekes. But pleasant gustatory surprises often awaited the wayfarer in sequestered places where a competent German hausfrau ruled the kitchen. In a letter to the Sheboygan Herald in 1913, a Civil War veteran states that he had come from the army weak and emaciated, but during the intensely cold winter of 1863-64, he slept warm in the comfortable beds of the German taverns of eastern Wisconsin and gained thirty pounds in six weeks on their substantial fare. This element also introduced delicatessen stores, now so numerous, a German word which means delicious "eats."

5. Education

> From 1780 to 1830 Germany has produced all the ideas of our historic age; and
> for half a century still, perhaps for a whole century, our great work will be to think
> them out again – thus at the end of the last century arose the philosophic German
> genius, which, having inaugurated a new metaphysics, theology, poetry, literature,
> linguistic science, an exegesis, erudition, descends now into the sciences, and
> continues its evolution. No more original spirit, more universal, more fertile in
> consequences of every scope and species, more capable of transforming and
> reforming everything, has appeared for 300 years. It is of the same order as that of
> the Renaissance and of the Classical Age. It, like them, connects itself with the great
> epochs of the world's history.

Thus wrote Henri Taine, the great French critic and historian, in 1864. See *Taine's History of English Literature*, p.374, vol. III, Henry Holt & Co., New York, 1877.

From kindergarten to university Wisconsin's educational system is greatly indebted to German influence. Not all of this influence is traceable to German residents of Wisconsin, far from it; it measurably due to the presence in the older states of German educators and former American students at German universities. Among the former were men of such far-reaching influence as Follen, Beck and Lieber; among the latter, Bache, Bancroft, Henry Barnard, Everett, Motley and Ticknor. Hence the public school system of Wisconsin, though brought into existence chiefly through the persistent efforts of Col. Michael Frank, a man of German stock, was, no doubt, a consequence of the discussion of the Prussian system in the East and its adoption by Massachusetts, Ohio and other states.

Impressed by the superiority of several German schools of Cincinnati, patterned after the Prussian system, Rev. Calvin Stowe, at the teachers' convention held at Columbus in 1836, made an address on "The Prussian System of Public Instruction and Its Application to the United States." As a consequence, Professor Stowe was sent abroad by Ohio and after studying the school systems of England, Scotland, France, the Netherlands, the German states; Denmark and Russia, he commended on his return the Prussian system as the best adapted to the United States, declaring it "as nearly complete as human ingenuity and skill can make it." He appended a translation of the school laws of Prussia to his report, and the school laws of Ohio were patterned accordingly after the Prussian system. According to G.

H. Martin's *Evolution of the Massachusetts Public School System*, the common schools of that state were at their lowest ebb about 1825. Through the influences noted above and the publication in New York in 1833 of the French Commissioner Cousin's favorable report on the Prussian system, the latter was adopted in Massachusetts in 1837 under the leadership of Horace Mann and Gov. Everett. But formidable efforts were made in the legislature of 1839 to repeal the new school law, which "was charged with trying to Prussianize the schools and to substitute for the democratic principles of the past the arbitrary methods of European despotism." But although the attempt failed, opposition did not cease, as a reference to the controversy between "The Association of Boston Masters (Boston, 1845) and Horace Mann" clearly shows. Indeed public free schools were decried as un-American as late as 1856 in a *Defense of the American Policy as Opposed to the Encroachments of Foreign Influence*, by Thomas R. Whitney, a book championing the principles of the American party. German Americans are therein severely criticized for advocating the education of poor children by the state, and the promotion of education by the introduction of the free school, with the power of forcing parents to send their children to school (pp.176-177).

Like the conservative element, both German Catholics and Lutherans did not favor the so-called "godless" public free schools for their members, hence they established parochial schools wherein their respective religious tenets and other branches were taught in the mother tongue, though seldom to the exclusion of the vernacular. Although handicapped by a dearth of teachers conversant with both languages, these churches had no objection to the teaching of English, but feared that the faith of their youth would be jeopardized by entrusting their education to a purely secular institution, the public school, sincerely believing that the supervision was the prerogative of the church and not that of the state. The liberals, on the other hand, believed in secular education and strongly advocated the establishment of public free schools. "A free-school system" was one of the demands of the "Forty-Eighters" in Rhenish-Bavaria, as is disclosed by the journal of Karl Krumrey, an elector of the revolutionary parliament, who afterward settled in Sheboygan County in 1849.

Yet, at a time when higher education was not generally considered the proper function of the state, they founded academies of their own, one of which still survives as the University School, Milwaukee, after more than seventy years of uninterrupted usefulness. Founded in 1851, it soon gained a high reputation for efficiency under its first principal, Peter Engelmann, trained pedagogue and political refugee from Rhenish-Bavaria, whose successful method of teaching was subsequently introduced into our public schools. Although Mrs. Carl Schurz, trained by Froebel himself, conducted the first kindergarten in the United States at Watertown, in 1855, Engelmann's German-English Academy was the first school in the state to introduce permanently this method of teaching beginners. Needless to say that it proved a success, for it was in accord with his system of teaching.

The teaching of singing, drawing and gymnastics also found its way into the public schools through German influence, as did domestic science and more recently vocational training and continuation schools. An ardent naturalist, Engelmann organized in 1858 a purely German natural history society. The resulting collection was installed in the Academy, where it continued its usefulness and donated to the city in 1882, whence dates Milwaukee's famous museum. Adjoining the University School were the German-American Teachers' Seminary and the Turners' Normal School, whose numerous graduates have for years plied their respective vocations in all parts of the country. Another liberal, whose remarkable personality exercised a wide influence, was Madame Francisca Anneke, writer, educator, feminist, and champion of human rights of international fame, who, after serving as military aide to her husband, Colonel Fritz Anneke, in the German revolution of 1848, fled with him to Milwaukee, where she long conducted a successful school for young ladies, which, like Engelmann's, was patronized by the best element, irrespective of nationality.

But throughout Wisconsin during its formative period there were scattered Germans of the highest culture who as clergymen, educators, physicians, druggists and teachers of drawing, music and languages, left their impress on their respective communities. Many, however, were compelled to take up other occupations. Some tried farming and were ridiculed as "Latin farmers," while others became colonized, like Dr. Karl Mieding, a former professor at Heidelberg, who, with the poet-merchant, Rudolph Puchner, founded New Holstein. Quite a number acquired such command of the English as to become prominent educators in our public schools. Among these was Theodore Bernhard of Watertown, a graduate of the University of Berlin, through whose initiative the free text books measure was enacted, and his city was the first in the state to supply free text books to the pupils of its public schools. Such were also Supt. H. O. R. Siefert and Principal Frederick Lau, of Milwaukee, both exceptionally successful educators. Modest, yet effective, was the influence of the German women who in those early days had classes of girls in sewing, knitting, crocheting, embroidery and other feminine crafts. Lack of proficiency in the vernacular, especially difficult of acquisition to an adult foreigner, and prejudice of the American, delayed for a time the Germans' general participation in public education; still, as early as 1843, we find Dr. Francis Huebschmann a member of the Milwaukee school board. Some of the educational achievements of the German churches have already been noticed.

The establishment of normal schools was successfully advocated in the East by the reformers mentioned above, and especially by Chas. Brooks, one of Prof. Follen's most enthusiastic pupils at Harvard. In spite of opposition and ridicule, they also brought about the introduction of the German method for teaching deaf-mutes oral speech. German universities were next to be copied, the University of Michigan, established in 1837, being the first of this type, but not until the opening of Johns Hopkins in 1876 was the plan fully realized. Technical, mining and agricultural schools, patterned after German institutions, came also in due time. But in order to fairly appreciate this revolution in American education under the influence of German institutions and scholars, one should read contemporary publications covering the subject.

Apart from the educators of our formative period who had come under the spell of German culture, the presence here of so many graduates of German universities undoubtedly contributed greatly to increase its potency. As early as 1851, Dr. Godfrey Aigner, a scholarly Viennese, was elected a member of the Board of Regents of our then infant State University. He was followed by Schurz, Edward Salomon and others. Like some other institutions of learning, the university would probably have been discontinued during the Civil War but for the efforts of Gov. Salomon. Since early in the fifties, there was a German on the meager faculty, but the scope of my sketch does not permit many details on this subject.

As an indication of what might be quoted, I refer to Dr. J. W. Hoyt's official Report on Education in Europe in the Transactions of the State Agricultural Society of Wisconsin for 1869. As U. S. Commissioner, Hoyt had visited the agricultural schools of Europe, and he awards the palm to Germany and Baron Liebig, on whose recommendation he studied the agricultural school in connection with the University of Jena. As editor, lecturer, and a man of great influence, he gave to Wisconsin what he had learned in Germany.

6. Temperance

Intemperance has been the bane of society since ancient times. The Nordics, especially were hard drinkers, hence their decedents in America came honestly by the pernicious habit. How best to combat the evil has engaged reformers for years. Some, like Gov. Patrick Henry of Virginia, recognizing the stubborn persistence of ancient social custom, sought to wean people from strong drink by introducing a milder beverage like beer; while others firmly believed that the only sure remedy is prohibition. The champions of the latter measure finally prevailed and prohibition is now one of our basic laws.

Before the Civil War whiskey was the popular stimulant, which the numerous small distillers sold as low as 12 ½ cents the gallon, and the taverns that lined the highways and the village streets dispensed at three cents the drink. There were also many stores which always had a barrel of whiskey on tap, with a convenient tin cup, where the customers could help themselves without charge – all of which was not conducive to temperance. Indeed, next to slavery, intemperance was the recognized national evil. George W. Julian, commenting on this evil in his *Political Recollections*, says that Congress ended March 3, 1851, in a drunken orgy. Although preponderantly opposed to prohibition, abundant evidence shows the German immigrants of that period less intemperate than most nationalities.

A. C. Wheeler says on this point in his *Chronicles of Milwaukee*, 1861, pp. 279-281: "Destitution when brought to public notice is found generally to be the result of intemperance, and it is no more than justice to say that the few cases that at intervals transpire are not among Germans." This condition was by no means due altogether to their partiality for beer, but it was a time-honored custom with them to imbibe it slowly, whether at meals or in public places. Whiskey was gulped down quickly, hence Americans wondered how two Germans could visit for an hour over a mug of beer. Moreover, according to the late Jeremiah Quinn of Milwaukee, and other keen observers, many German public houses of the time were more like social clubs, where neighbors met in friendly converse, discussing around tables the questions of the day, or playing cards; each partaking of refreshments according to his individual desire, and settling his own score.

The hosts, often men of consequence, perhaps prominent political refugees, or scholars unable to capitalize their German learning, jealously guarded the reputation of their places. But the spread of the pernicious American habit of treating, agreeably to which a man is expected to "treat" as often as he is "treated," together with the subsequent organization of the liquor traffic, counteracted greatly the bettering influence of German social custom. Now nearly obsolete, their rational habit of ordering refreshments is recalled by the phrase, "Let's Dutch it," used occasionally by some sensible person proposing that each pay for his own score. If criminal statistics are a criterion of temperance, as is alleged, then Wisconsin, at a time when the influence of persons of German birth was at its height, compares favorably with Maine, a state devoid of this element. According to these statistics, the ration of convicts per million inhabitants in Wisconsin was 455 in 1860, 396 in 1879, and 448 in 1880; while Maine had 406 in 1860, 592 in 1870, and 624 in 1880.

7. Business

There is hardly a single line of business or craftsmanship in which the Germans of Wisconsin have not distinguished themselves, hence it is almost redundant to enumerate any; yet a few in which they have been exceptionally prominent, or the unusual, will be mentioned. The blacksmith, wheelwright, and miller were indispensable craftsmen in pioneer days and abundant data in my possession show the Germans well represented among these from the very beginning. They formed likewise a large proportion of the early carpenters, masons, harness makers, coopers, tailors and shoemakers. The versatile Yankee could turn his hand to anything, but where skill could only be acquired by a long apprenticeship, he was usually deficient; hence it is not surprising that the early jewelers, bakers (confectioners), potters, cabinet makers, etc., were chiefly Germans. This was true even in then such American communities as Berlin, Ripon, Waupun, Horicon, Waukesha and Whitewater, which, in 1858, boasted of sixteen cabinet makers, all but one of whom were Germans.

The manufacture of aluminum products, in which Wisconsin leads the country, was started at Two Rivers by Joseph Koenig, who is still active in the management of his large plant, now a unit of the Aluminum Goods Company of America (a $12,000,000 corporation), of which George Vits, of the mammoth Manitowoc unit, is president. Conrad Werra, of the Werra Aluminum foundry, and President A. C. Pankratz of the Quality Aluminum Foundry Co., Waukesha, and the Wentorf brothers, of the West Bend Aluminum Co., were likewise pioneers in this industry who gained their experience at Two Rivers. Men of German stock also dominate the manufacture of enameled ware in the state and country, the most notable being the great establishments of the Volraths at Sheboygan, Kohler at Kohler, the Kieckhefers and Geuder, Paeschke & Frey Co., of Milwaukee. They also lead in the manufacture of candy, naming only Eline and Ziegler of Milwaukee, Funke of La Crosse, and Brenner of Green Bay. They likewise lead in cheese making, and fairly monopolize the manufacture of cigars in the state. In coal, the names of Reiss of Sheboygan and elsewhere, Uhrig of Milwaukee, have long been pre-eminent. Ringling Brothers, Baraboo's seven famous sons who became the world's greatest showmen, were of German parentage.

While Barnum, whose show they later absorbed, held the American people like to be humbugged, the Ringlings won the confidence of the public by living up to their representations, by raising the standard of their circus, by barring preying camp-followers, and by more efficient management. The German element is also in control of the wholesale dry goods houses of the state, the three leaders being Goll & Frank Co., and H. Stern, Jr., & Bro. Co., both established in 1850, and Landauer & Co., originating in 1867–all of Milwaukee. For seventy years German names have predominated in the manufacture of apparel, Friend Brothers, now discontinued, David Adler & Sons, and Rice and Friedman, of Milwaukee, being the most important. The wholesale millinery houses of the state have also been in the hands of this stock, as the names of Blumenfeld, Locher, Heyman and Gens indicate.

For fifty years have they likewise been dominant factors in the wholesale hardware trade, the names of Pritzlaff, Frankfurth, Suelflohn & Seefeld and Gross of Milwaukee, and Kroner of La Crosse, being the most noted. Although not especially partial to lumber, we find such names as Frederick Weyerhaeuser, at his death America's greatest operator; Anton Klaus of Green Bay, one time shingle king, and C. J. L. Meyer of Fond du Lac, whose immense sash, door and blind factory was considered the largest in the world fifty years ago. Meyer was likewise the leading factor in building the Air Line, now a branch of the C. & N. W., to Milwaukee. In recent years Schlesinger ranked highest in the mining industry, but of more far-reaching influence on the state were Hegler and Matthiessen, two young mining engineers from Freiberg, who came to Mineral Point in 1858 to study the zinc ore situation. Thereupon they established a successful zinc smeltery at La Salle, Ill., the seat of coal and fire clay. As a consequence, what was formerly refuse at the mines, rose to $10 and $15 a ton, which meant millions to southwestern Wisconsin.

Germans also comprise a majority of the numerous shoe manufacturers of the state, these being among the leaders: Weinbrenner, Mayer, Casper, Ebner, Helmholtz, Luedke, Ortgiesen, Rich, Ripple, Rohn and Schoenecker of Milwaukee, Kieckhefer of Fond du Lac, Fiebrich-Hilker of Racine, Jung of Sheboygan, Pentler of Wausau and Wolfram of Madison, Lake Mills, Waterloo and Watertown. They outclass in fine sausage, naming only Usinger, Weisel and Frank of Milwaukee, whose product sells all over the land. As makers of hosiery they command in state and nation, Gardner heading the vast Phoenix plants and Freschl the Holeproof factories. They outrank in church furniture, the largest plant being that of Chas. F. Schuetze of Waukesha.

The Earlings, sons of German parents, have distinguished themselves in transportation. Guido Pfister, highly successful in tanning and banking, promoted and built the Milwaukee & Northern Ry., now the Superior division of the C. M. & St. P. Railway. Col. W. H. Jacobs, prominent in banking and other enterprises, was one of the principal promoters of the Wisconsin Central Ry., now the Soo. The Germans have also been commanding figures in the tanning industry, the names of Pfister, Vogel, Gallun and Trostel of Milwaukee, Eisendrath of Racine, Roenitz of Sheboygan and Rueping of Fond du Lac, being the most prominent.

They are likewise leaders in the manufacture of engines, machinery and ranges, these names being especially conspicuous: Falk, John, Harnischfeger, Hoffman, Kieckhefer, Koehring, Lindemann, Logemann and Vilter of Milwaukee; Steinle of Madison; Kahlenberg of Two Rivers, and Studemann of Sheboygan. The manufacture of musical instruments is in their hands, including the building of church organs. Adolph Meinecke of Milwaukee was the pioneer toy manufacturer of the state a business still conducted by his grandsons.

The first lager beer brewery in Wisconsin was established by a German in Milwaukee in 1841. The Bests, founders of the great Pabst Brewing Co., began in 1842, while August Krug started in 1848, the business later famous as the Joseph Schlitz Brewing Co. Valentine Blatz began brewing in Milwaukee in 1851, Adam Gettelmann in 1854, Fred Miller in 1855, and Franz Falk in 1856. These establishments, aided by the wonderful executive ability of Capt Fred Pabst, and the Uihleins of the Schlitz Brewing Co., made Milwaukee beer famous and popular the world over. Many other places in the state had lager beer breweries, usually supplying the local wants; but some like the John Gund Brewing Co., C. and J. Michels and Heilemann of La Crosse, Schreier and Gutsch of Sheboygan, Rahr of Manitowoc and Hagemeister of Green Bay, did of considerable magnitude, has been in control of this element. It is also pertinent to mention that the wonderful success of some of these brewers found expression not alone in huge breweries and palatial homes, but also in the erection of hotels, restaurants, theaters and business blocks, the establishment of banks, and in generous benefactions. Since a product reflects the character of its maker, the high quality of Wisconsin manufactures has justly been attributed to the notable traits of its large German element.

8. Music

"One remarkable fact in the Reformation psalmody is this: The Lutherans cultivated harmony, which Calvin did not." James Warrington.

"The English," says A. E. Bostwick in *The Different West*, "are probably the most unmusical nation on earth; what hope there is for us Americans we have largely from the leaven of other peoples that has been and is working on us."

"American music was first planted in very sterile soil; both Pilgrims and Puritans were opposed to the development of the musical art!" *The National Music of America*, Louis A. Elson (Boston, 1900).

Even church organs were opposed as "popish" in New England, and it was not until 1790 that this wonderful instrument was introduced into a Congregational church in Boston, with a German as organist. It is therefore, not surprising that the musical Germans – Lutherans, Catholics, Freethinkers, et al – reacted favorably on their native neighbors in pioneer Wisconsin. They all sang, even while at work in house, shop, or field; and on Sundays while visiting, men, women and children sang joyously their German hymns and folk-songs. The Catholics especially had fine choirs which early rendered classical church music, and leading Irish churches were served by German organists. Many played musical instruments, and as early as 1842 Milwaukee boasted a fine German band, while Hess' orchestra had the call at American dancing parties. But there were also amateurs of great talent, both vocal and instrumental, among men and women of the highest culture, and in 1850 these were organized into the Milwaukee Musical Society which, within a short time, gave excellent concerts, even operas, under their able, enthusiastic director, Hans Balatka.

Their productions amazed the entire country and brought the highest praise even from the metropolitan press of the east. In 1855 there arrived Christian Bach, composer, arranger and director, who organized Bach's famous orchestra. His compositions, like those of Kaun and other Milwaukee composers of German stock, found favor even in the best musical centers of Europe. Numerous other musical societies were organized here and elsewhere in the state, whose concerts and song festivals were generally patronized, resulting in the first social rapprochement between Yankee and Teuton. A study of the programs of these musical societies, quite a number of which still flourish, must convince even a tyro of their great cultural influence.

They made a profound impression on the native element which, twenty-five years after the organization of the Milwaukee Musical Society, founded the Arion Society. But even this excellent society has had German directors and members. Among their numerous teachers of music there were also men of outstanding ability, such as Bruening, Drobegg, Luening and von Gumpert. Undoubtedly the greatest musical event in the history of

Wisconsin was the North-American Saengerfest, held in Milwaukee in 1886, after three years of painstaking preparation under the direction of Prof. Ernst Catenhusen. The classical program of seven concerts consisting of sixty-five numbers was rendered perfectly by a mass chorus of 2,500 voices recruited from eighty-five visiting societies; a mixed choir of 1,000 local singers and 800 children, with a selected orchestra of 100 pieces, and some of the world's most famous soloists. Two hundred musical critics, representing both hemispheres, were in attendance. But this is not the whole story. Items in the country press of fifty to seventy years ago speak of the return of German musicians from study at Leipsic or Berlin; of successful concerts by local or visiting German talent, of German music teachers. Song books of the period were profuse with gems of the German Lied; while some of the hymns used in the American churches and in the ritual of secret societies were borrowed from the German.

9. The Bar

Although not without its prominent representatives at the bar, the German element of Wisconsin has never filled its proportionate quota in the legal profession. Apart from the handicap of language in the first generation, the German lacks the forensic ability, bearing, and astuteness of the Yankee; the assurance, blarney, and cunning of the Irish – qualities that impress public and jury. In painstaking research and the accurate marshaling of facts, the German was unsurpassed; but ordinarily he was too honest, too blunt, to make a highly successful trial lawyer. Still, the race boasts of some eminent members of the Wisconsin bar. Bouck, Bragg, Felker, Fethers, Mann, Noggle, Sharpstein, and Woodward were of mixed Anglo-German ancestry. F. W. Von Cotzhausen, Gov. Salomon and Gen. Winkler ranked among the foremost lawyers of the state; while Col. Krez, Merton, Rietbrock, Wahl and Weisbrod were attorneys of great ability. The German lawyer should make a good judge, and quite a number have honored the Wisconsin bench. While the ratio of lawyers of German descent is now considerably larger and their limitations less than formerly, I dare not venture an opinion as to their comparative standing.

10. Medicine

It goes without saying that the German element of the state has also distinguished itself in medicine, surgery and pharmacy. The coming of Dr. Francis Huebschmann, in 1842, marks the beginning of the influx of German physicians, graduates of famous German universities, whose culture and professional skill enriched Wisconsin at a time when native practitioners were often handicapped by indifferent training. "In 1850, out of sixty persons engaged in the practice of medicine in the counties of Grant, Iowa, and LaFayette, only twelve were entitled to be called 'doctors'." *Wisconsin Magazine of History*, December 1923. Among the more noteworthy arrivals before 1850 were Doctors Aigner, Fessel, Jung, Kalckhoff, Luening, Sauerhering, Stadler, Wunderly, Wunsch and Rosenthal, the last a successful surgeon employing original methods. Dr. Harpke, who had majored in ophthalmology at Wuerzburg and Berlin, was Milwaukee's first eye specialist, coming in 1851.

During the Civil War some of these and many other well-trained German physicians gave their services to their adopted county, among them being Dr. Emanuel Munck, later of Fond du Lac, who was the first preceptor of Dr. Nicholas Senn, also of pure German stock, who became one of the world's greatest surgeons. Senn was equally great as a teacher and writer in his profession, upon which his influence was incalculable. Many of the original surgical procedures which his genius evolved were first applied practically while he was chief of staff of a Milwaukee hospital. He became professor of Anatomy and Surgery in Rush Medical College, Chicago, and surgeon general of Wisconsin and Illinois regiments during the Spanish-American War. Scarcely lower in the hall of surgical fame stands Dr. Albert J. Ochsner, a native of Sauk county, but for years of Chicago and the world. He has been officially recognized by the University of Wisconsin as one of her most distinguished graduates. Another specialist of international fame is Dr. Joseph Schneider, likewise a graduate of Wuerzburg, who has made Milwaukee the Mecca of those afflicted with eye trouble.

III. Social, Political and Cultural Life

1. Politics

"Wir sind ein unpolitisches Volk" – "We are an unpolitical people." – Prince Buelow.

In politics the Germans of Wisconsin have not exercised an influence commensurate with their numbers. Apart from the handicap of language and their lack of political experience, they have been no match for the Yankee, to whom politics was formerly a pastime from youth to old age. Besides, those of English speech were prejudiced against "foreigners," whose language, type and ways were a provocation and a mark of inferiority to them. Still, Germans would have been more successful in winning political preferment, did they possess the solidarity of certain other ethnic elements. But even this does not altogether account for the comparative paucity of office holders among them. Experience has shown that even when aroused to more united action, they are indifferent to spoils. Such was the case during the Bennett Law agitation, and it was so in 1920, when Paul Reinsch, the son of a Lutheran clergyman and one of our greatest men, was the democratic candidate for United States senator and ran a poor third. In spite of all this, their influence has by no means been inconsiderable.

Before the birth of the republican party, in 1854, the Germans of the state were almost solidly democrats, not merely because the name and personnel of that party attracted them, but because the Whigs had generally opposed granting foreigners an early franchise; had favored drastic temperance legislation, and were suspected of knownothingism. When slavery became the all-absorbing issue, a majority of the liberals and Evangelicals, and some Lutherans and Reformed allied themselves with the republican party, becoming strong factors therein. Although no other ethnic element in this country was so unanimous against slavery (Grimshaw), such an unbridgeable chasm separated the liberals from the conservatives, especially the Catholics, that a political union was impossible.

During the revolution in the German states in 1848, when the liberals demanded unification, representative government, and other democratic reforms, the orthodox churches opposed these and upheld the autocratic rulers from whom they derived their sustenance. This, together with the heretical views held by the liberals, resulted here in bitter controversy, ending in irreconcilable antipathies. Moreover, the democratic party had early given substantial recognition to the Germans, even to the extent of a state treasurer; had fostered their press and championed their cause, resulting in organization, party loyalty, and self-interest, which the natural aversion to slavery could not displace. However, although the majority of the Germans continued loyal to the democratic party, the defection of so large a number of intelligent, enthusiastic, militant members turned the scales and made Wisconsin a republican state.

In recognition of this powerful accession, the republicans, in 1857, nominated Carl Schurz for lieutenant governor. Owing to the railroad scandal of the Bashford administration, the election that year proved exceedingly close; still it is significant that the German candidate on each state ticket met with defeat. Yet, though Carl Schurz was rejected through the prejudice of the electorate, he served as chairman of the Wisconsin delegation to the national republican convention in 1860; became one of the most powerful campaign speakers in the country in both German and English; was appointed minister to Spain and a major general during the Civil War; served with distinction as United States senator from Missouri and as a member of President Hayes' cabinet; later becoming an editor and author of world-wide fame. Can any other Wisconsin man match this extraordinary record? On the other hand, the eloquent Dr. Huebschmann, who in the constitutional convention of 1846 had been the successful champion of granting foreigners the franchise after a residence in the state of one year, remained loyal to the democratic party, which he had served twice as presidential elector, and as superintendent of Indian affairs. In the Civil War, in every crisis the German element exercised a powerful influence in behalf of the right. When the issue of greenbacks, in the '70s, and the free coinage of silver, in 1896, were offered as a panacea for financial ills, the election returns show that the Germans of Wisconsin came out strongly for sound money.

In 1890 and 1892 large numbers of Germans, notably the Lutherans, changed their party allegiance on the Bennett law issue, thereby throwing the republicans from power and giving the state's electoral vote to the democrats. The law appeared to many, like myself, merely an act to insure every Wisconsin child an opportunity to learn English; but the clergy of both German Catholic and Lutheran churches held that it meant also giving the state control over parochial schools. In the light of recent legislation in other states, their fears may have been justified. It should be observed, however, that although the Bennett law was repealed through their influence, the English language has not been neglected in these schools. In this connection it is pertinent to mention that in 1888 the German Society of Milwaukee, then including representative citizens of that nationality irrespective of creed, memorialized congress for the enactment of a uniform system of suffrage laws throughout the country, requiring a five years' residence here before this "high prerogative" be granted foreigners. They also protested against any state granting foreigners the right to vote and hold office before these conditions are complied with. Wisconsin has had only two chief executives of German stock, Edward Salomon and Emanuel L. Phillip. Both were war governors who acquitted themselves with exceptional ability. However, at least two other Germans might have had the honor, Capt. Fred Pabst and John C. Koch, both popular, wealthy business men. The "organization" wanted them to run, when a nomination was equivalent to an election.

On several occasions, when the prospects for success were not inviting, the democrats nominated men of this stock for governor and United States senator, but the election returns showed no serious inroads on the republican majority. Paul Husting was the only man of German strain to represent Wisconsin in the United States senate. His father was a German, his mother of French and Indian stock. He knew German thoroughly. Congressmen Bouck, Bragg, Winans and Woodward were partly of German descent. The following were of German birth or parentage: Barwig, Berger, Brickner, Deuster, Esch, Guenther, Kopp, Kuestermann, Lampert, Otjen, Sauerhering, Schafer, Schneider, Henry Smith, Voigt and Weisse. Hon. John J. Esch, republican, now a member of the Interstate Commerce Commission, long represented the La Crosse district in Congress, where he achieved fame as the joint author of the Esch-Cummins Law, a measure of great importance and subject of continued controversy. Hon. Richard Guenther, republican, originally a leader of the Oshkosh Turner Society, after serving two terms as state treasurer, was elected for three terms in the sixth congressional district, and failing of a renomination, went into the adjoining strongly democratic district and won a signal victory. He closed his long public career as United States consul in Europe. Hon. Florian Lampert, also of Oshkosh, had five sons in the world war. Henry Smith, Labor, had but one term in congress, but he served the city of Milwaukee officially for fifty years, dying poor in worldly goods, but rich in the esteem of his fellowmen.

The State Supreme Court has had three members of German parentage: Judges Siebecker, Eschweiler and Doerfler, the first named being chief justice at the time of his death. Federal Judge Ferdinand Geiger is the son of a German pioneer of Grant county. Beginning in 1852, party conventions usually gave the Germans a place on the state ticket, but with the advent of the primary elections they did not always fare so well. However, in 1924, they gained two places, Lt. Gov. Henry Huber and Secretary of State Fred L. Zimmerman. Several men of German stock have also served as foreign ministers, the most noteworthy being Schurz and the late Dr. Paul Reinsch, ambassador to China. Another man who has greatly distinguished himself in the service of his state and country is Dr. B. H. Meyer, chairman of the Interstate Commerce Commission. Rear Admiral Albert Mertz was the son of a Dodge County pioneer. The Germans were prominent factors in the progressive movement from the beginning, such aggressive leaders as Baumgartner, Bosshard, Cochems, Dithmar, Doerfler, Gaffron, Gross, Host, Kronshage, Krumrey, Mauthe and Zentner swinging the German republican counties into line for La Follette and progressive legislation. Baensch, Fink, Pfister, Phillip and Winkler were leading figures among the conservative republicans. Cotzhausen, Deuster, Horn, Huebschmann, Husting, Krez, Kuehn, Lueck, the Ringles, Rodolf, Carl Schmidt, Schmitz, Schoeffel, Weisbrod and Weisse were prominent in the councils of the democratic party. Victor Berger has for years been the leader of the Wisconsin socialists. Mayor Dan Hoan is of German descent through his mother.

2. Social Activities and Amusements

"We have gone amusement mad as a nation," said Henry M. Leland in 1923. But it was not always thus. Writing from Wisconsin in 1850, Fredrika Bremer, the famous Swedish novelist, then touring in the country, said of the Milwaukee Germans: "Their music and dances and other popular pleasures distinguish them from the Anglo-American people, who, particularly in the west, have no other pleasures than 'business'!" Writing from Madison, October 5, 1850, she comments further:

The weather was bright and sunny, although cold, and I wished to avail myself of the afternoon for an excursion on the beautiful lake. But it is Sunday, and Sundays people must not amuse themselves, not even in God's beautiful scenery. But sleep in church – that you may do.

According to Governor Bradford and other authorities the Puritans of New England adjusted their lives to the Old Testament, to the draconic laws of Leviticus. Not so with the Germans and other continental peoples, who had lived for more than one thousand years according to Christianity's mild interpretation of the New Dispensation, which was also the custom in "Merrie Old England" until the triumph of puritanism in 1640 put the lid on its merriness. Yet there were some week-day amusements among the natives of early Wisconsin, such as bees, square-dances, horse racing, hunting, fishing, riding, skating, horse-play, charades, puppet and wax figure shows, a stray concert or lecture, and once a year the circus at the county seat; while the men played poker or seven-up in the numerous taverns in those very wet days.

But most of these amusements were not countenanced by the godly, but denounced as wicked, especially the round dances of German origin, which were considered unspeakably bad. The social activities were, therefore, considered very bad, especially because they "desecrated" the Hebraic Sabbath with some of these pleasures. Here is what A. C. Wheeler says in his *Chronicles of Milwaukee*, in 1861:

> The influx of this nation has resulted in the giving of two or three distinctive characteristics to the town. With them they brought their love of music, their sociability, and their beer drinking habits. Although all have assimilated with the Americans and have learned the English language, still the more admirable traits have not been relinquished, but seem to have given tone to the town.

This appreciation of the salutary influence of German social custom is voiced also by *Harper's Magazine* of 1881. It says:

> But with the Germans came the German ability of enjoyment through cheap and innocent amusements. In the fatherland they had been accustomed to go with wife and children to the garden and open air cafes, where the father placidly smoked his pipe and sipped his beer, while the mother quietly plied her needles or knitting, and the children played around her or strolled about and chatted with each other, while all listened to the charming music discoursed by good bands.

We owe to them also certain games at cards, such as schafskopf, sixty-six, pinochle, solo and that most scientific of all card games, skat, which has reacted even on the Brahmin, whist resulting in bridge. The Christmas tree, Kriskinkle (Christkindel, meaning Christ child), the Easter egg, the Easter rabbit, all were brought to Wisconsin by the Germans. The ladies introduced the Kaffeeklatsch, social afternoon gatherings not yet extinct. The men also popularized certain games, such as bowling. And they were greatly given to organizing sharpshooters' societies. All of these amusements were, however, enjoyed without hurry, yet with keen delight, with – there is but one word for it – **Gemuethelichkeit**. There was no such mad rush as we see now.

3. The German Press

Since the millions of non-British foreigners who have come to our shores can not learn in a trice a speech so difficult as English, a foreign language press is necessary to acquaint these newcomers with the principles and the laws of this government, to teach them their duties here, and to explain the questions of the day. Naturally, these papers also carry news and literary items from their respective fatherlands, for, being human and of foreign culture, the first generation of readers will continue to be interested in their relatives, friends, and early environments abroad. Their children, however, generally prefer to read papers printed in the vernacular, hence the foreign language press is sure to die sooner or later. The *Wisconsin Banner*, democratic, was the first German paper published in the state, making its appearance in Milwaukee in 1844, when the city had a population of 6,400.

The editor, Moritz Schoeffler, was a strong, influential man, who continued at its helm for thirty years. Since that early day a large number of German papers have made their appearance in the state representing the various political or religious opinions held by this element, but mention must be confined to a few of the most important. One of these was *Der Seebote*, Whig at the start, then always strongly democratic, which was edited for a long time by P. V. Deuster. Another was *Der Volksfreund*, also democratic, later consolidated with the *Banner*. Bernhard Domschke established the first German republican paper in Milwaukee, after a few years of hard struggle becoming associated with W. W. Coleman (a German) in conducting the *Herold*, subsequently one of the most successful and influential German papers in the country.

Domschke, was an unusually gifted writer and speaker in the anti-slavery cause, was of such intense confictions, that, at the outbreak of the Civil War, he enlisted and saw three years of hard service, being wounded, captured, and long confined in Libby Prison. However, he was not the only German editor who forsook the pen for the musket. Carl H. Schmidt, who had founded the *Nordwesten* at Manitowoc in 1855, suspended his paper to serve four years in the Civil War, after which he re-established it. Another prominent champion of freedom was Carl Roeser, who founded the *Wisconsin Demokrat* at Manitowoc in 1853, a German free soil organ. Editor Otto Troemel, also of that city, likewise served in that war. And so did Capt. A. R. Marschner, a Sheboygan editor. Carl Zillier, who began his editorial functions in the same city in 1857, spoke and wrote German and English with equal facility, his influential activity extending over a period of sixty years. D. Blumenfeld, of the Watertown *Weltbuerger*, founded in 1857, conducted it successfully from 1859 till his death in 1905. An influential German paper of large circulation was the *Dodge County Pionier* of Mayville, which espoused the cause of sound money in 1896, thereby helping to turn that hitherto democratic stronghold to the republicans.

Another influential paper has been the *Nordstern*, of La Crosse. Its leading editors have been John Ulrich, A. Steinlein and Adolph Candrian. In 1873, the German Protestant Printing Association of Milwaukee began the publication of the weekly *Germania*, independent politically but with a Protestant (Lutheran) christian tendency. However, the venture soon passed into the control of George Brumder, an Alsatian, who achieved a phenomenal success, adding other publications, including the daily *Herold* and other papers owned by the Colemans. He was especially fortunate in his editor-in chief, George Koeppen, the nobility of whose character and attainments was matched by his noble birth, for he was, in reality, a German count, having dropped the title and name when he became an American. His effective leaders and conduct of the paper elevated his readers and also led many of them into the republican fold. Other Milwaukee editors of note were Herman Sigel and C. H. Boppe. The *Herold, Germania*, etc., also published agricultural papers or supplements, with a large circulation and able editors.

Among these was former Lt. Gov. Francis Hoffmann, who had been prominent in the anti-slavery movement in Chicago, both as a writer and speaker, but who later conducted a model farm near Jefferson. He wrote for the Brumder publications under the pseudonym of "Hans Buschbauer," while his cultured wife contributed articles on domestic science under the name of "Grete." As to the great war, says Pixley's *Wisconsin in the World War:* "It is to the credit of the German press that they gave space to all war activities." They also published German plate matter, prepared by the University, and the State Council of Defense circulated a leader printed by the Milwaukee *Herold*, Grant, the son of whose editor, Gustav Haas, served overseas, fighting against his own cousins. Men of German stock have also been successful on the English press, naming only the Bleyers, Kronshage, and Berger of Milwaukee; the Rindlaubs of Platteville; the Roethes of Fennimore; Ringle of Wausau; Brandenburg of Madison; Gaffron of Plymouth; Lange of Fond du Lac, and Zander of Brillion.

4. Letters

The German element has likewise made valuable literary contributions, both in English and German, in prose and poetry; in fiction and history, in politics and education, in science and religion. The contributions of Protestant divine and Catholic dignitary, as well as those of secular writers, are far too numerous to mention, even the more important. Yet it seems fitting to single out Henry Nehrling's *The Birds of America*, an ornithological treatise of international reputation, published both in English and German. Perhaps mention should also be made of Schurz" campaign speeches, published in 1865. They are classics that compare with the best similar efforts of American statesmen. During the golden period of German influence in the third quarter of the past century, when Milwaukee was deservedly known for its German culture, Wisconsin harbored a number of German poets whose effusions found favor even in the Fatherland.

Indeed, it is the humble opinion of the writer that nothing that has been published by any Wisconsin poet in English will compare with some of the gems of several of these authors. One of the most noted of these poets was

Col. Conrad Krez, whose poem, "An Mein Vaterland," won the first prize in Leipzig against a thousand contestants. In justice to the poet, it should be said that he did not compose it expressly for the contest, for it was the spontaneous, heart-breaking plaint of a political exile, who loved his fatherland despite his faults and cruelty to him. Since the German Pegasus had many followers in the state, these names must suffice: Messrs. Dilg, von Ende, Gugler, Maerklin, Ruhland, Soubron, Thormaehlen, Zuendt and Dr. Curt Baum, and Mmes. Anneke, von Ende, and Fiebing, of Milwaukee; Messrs. Steinlein and Ulrich of La Crosse; Pflaum, Wallich, Wintermeier and Mrs. Wittmann of Manitowoc; Mr. Giegold of Marinette; Puchner of New Holstein; Sophie Gudden of Oshkosh, and Col. Krez of Sheboygan.

5. Sports

The gymnastic exercises for developing bodily strength and agility, introduced by the Turners, also included boxing, fencing, jumping, running, swimming, vaulting and wrestling but not all of the games embraced in the term "athletics" now, seemingly, the chief aim of our schools of higher education. Before the days of athletic clubs and public beaches, the Germans of the state had swimming schools, where many a boy and girl earned the distinction of "freigeschwommen," or winning their freedom from further supervision. The Turners were good wrestlers and some of them turned professional. Thus one of their number was a champion broadswordsman. The recent heavy weight champion wrestler, known as "Strangler Lewis," is of Wisconsin German stock. Badger boys of German extraction take to the American game of baseball and boast of such major league stars of the past as pitchers Eddie Joss, "Pete" Husting and Gus Krock; catcher Carisch, and such hitters as Otto Schomberg, Luderus, Merkle and Mollwitz.

They also take to college athletics, as the roster of any team, past or present will disclose. Such outstanding names as Cochems, Hahn, Kraenzlein, Osthoff, Remp, Schardt, and "Jumbo" Stiehm, can be matched by others. Some of these were prize winners in the world's Olympic games. Kraenzlein won the high hurdles at Paris in 1900, and held for some years the world's record on the broad jump. Archie Hahn, representing the Milwaukee Athletic Club, equaled the world's record of 9 3/5 for the century and won the 100 and 200 meter races at Athens. Arlie Schardt is a more recent Olympic star, winning at a later meet the third prize in the 3,000 meter race from a field of the world's fastest runners. Representatives of this element have also distinguished themselves as coaches, few men having been as successful as Bob Zuppke, whom sport writers have called the "Miracle Man of Football."

6. Thrift

Admonished by Holy Writ and by monitors and governments unto this day to practice thrift, those who heed the lessons are usually ridiculed. German thrift and success have, therefore, often been explained by the derisive statement: "A Dutchman will make a living where a white man will starve." Yet, very likely, the sarcastic critic was a wasteful man, who spent most of his time minding other people's business; while the object of his sarcasm attended strictly to his work, took care of everything, even to his payments, lived and dressed plainly but comfortably. The Germans all worked. As soon as a child was old enough, it had to help, the regular performance of such duties giving it a training which proved invaluable in later years. The women not only reared large families, but helped on the farm.

Take a typical case, that of my neighbor, Fred Honeyager, a retired farmer. His folks came over in 1854 with seven children on borrowed money. They soon rented a farm with only the slightest improvements, where three more children were born. Later the farm was bought on time, and the whole family, working together, soon paid for it. They had plenty of nourishing food, plain, substantial apparel, and such luxuries as forest and stream, garden and orchard yielded. All the children turned in their earnings, less a little spending money, until they were of age. Needless to say, that, with such training, they all in time acquired farms for themselves. In spite of their thrift and hard work, the parents lived to a happy old age, both dying at eighty-eight. However, lest this might be interpreted that all German thrift turns to things material, the record of another large family is herewith given, that of Henry Meyer, who located with his father in the Town of Mequon, now Ozaukee County, in 1842. He was a man of Herculean strength, who in harvest time, sometimes worked night and day;

still he had time to take a lively interest in church and public school, in farm improvement and local government. He was married twice, twelve children blessing the two unions. Dying when past eighty, he was survived by his second wife, who had borne him nine children. Charles, Henry and Oscar (Meyer) had a district school education and became successful business men. Arthur W., anatomist, B. S. University of Wisconsin, and M.D. of Johns Hopkins, is professor of human anatomy at Leland Stanford, and an author of note. Balthasar H., economist, a graduate of Oshkosh Normal, B. L. and Ph.D. University of Wisconsin and graduate courses at Berlin, was professor of political science at his alma mater, and is now chairman of the Interstate Commerce Commission. August, a mechanical engineer and a patentee of many devices, was educated at a business college and correspondence school. Martin, who took the short course at the University of Wisconsin, is the western representative of the Chris. Hansen Laboratories. Lisette and Minna, after graduating at the Oshkosh Normal, taught school and then married. Ernst, a graduate of the University of Wisconsin and Leipzig, is now director of surveys of the international Board of Health, Rockefeller Foundation, etc. Adolph, a graduate of the Oshkosh Normal and the University of Wisconsin, is professor of English at the University of Minnesota, consulting engineer, an authority on concrete, author and inventor of the Meyer governor, a fundamental patent in the paper industry. Lydia, after graduating at the University of Wisconsin and taking her M. A. at Leland Stanford, became a high school teacher in California.

Paraphrasing Cornelia, the German mothers of Wisconsin can well exclaim: "Here are my contributions."

7. Place Names and Patronymics

Notwithstanding the great volume of German immigration to Wisconsin in pioneer days, Teutonic place names are comparatively few in the state. Some of them, like Berlin, New Berlin, and Hanover, were so named by Yankees after their former homes in the east. In this connection it is well to remember that most German place names in New England and many in the south, such as Berlin, Brunswick, Hanover, and Mecklenburg, were given in admiration of the royal family of England and the states and cities of their origin. On the other hand, such points as Ableman, Mauston, Rhinelander, and Shullsburg, received their appellations in honor of men of German strain more or less remote. Again, in some instances, the original designations were later changed to English names, Hersheyville being thus turned to Hartland, Hamburg to Graffton, and Schwarzburg to North Milwaukee; while "Zum Braunen Hirsch," the name of a tavern, was translated to Brown Deer. Others were found objectionable on account of their jaw-breaking length. Such was that most atrocious German place name, Schleisingerville, so called after its Alsatian founder, and which was for years known locally as "Slinger," but was not officially changed to this form until recently.

The German founders sometimes deliberately selected non-German names, as was the case with Cedarburg. German Catholic settlements were often named after the patron saint of the church, and all but a few places in the state named after saints were settled by Catholic Germans. Holy Cross, Johnsburg, Lake Church, Marytown and Mt. Calvary are likewise such settlements. Some places were named after their founders, examples of such being Kohler, Kellnersville and Weyerhauser. Fussville was not an early seat of trouble, but was named after its founder, one Fuss, pronounced "foos," and meaning "foot." Naturally, a number were named after places and states in Germany and Switzerland, such as Kiel, New Holstein, New Glarus, and Wittenberg.

New Munster was not named after one of the provinces of Ireland but after Münster, in Westphalia, the former home of the original settlers. The names of German-American patriots are preserved in Blenker, Custer, Sigel, and Steuben. Marathon County has the largest number of townships with German names, thirteen, while Oneida, Shawano and Sheboygan have three each; Chippewa, Clark, Marinette, Taylor and Wood have two each, and twenty other counties have one each. The comparative rarity of German place names in a state peopled so largely by Germans is partly due to their indifference or unfamiliarity of procedure, but chiefly to the ambition of the "masterful" Yankee, who was often their friend and advisor. Thus Howard's Grove was named after the only Yankee in the place. Altogether there are about two hundred and eighty-five German place names in the state.

Recent writers have tried to establish the ratio of English stock in America in 1790, by the census of that year, although thousands of the names therein recorded were foreign patronymics spelled phonetically, or which had been anglicized by alteration or translation. Prior to 1850, the

United States census did not indicate the nationality of the population, and the original reports of Waukesha County for that year, which I have carefully studied, show conclusively that the names as entered are no guide to nationality. That of 1850, taken by George Pratt, mutilated German names frightfully, fully 75% being entered incorrectly, and fully 40% being recorded as English names. Thus Hauert was written Howard; Ochsner as Auctioner; Naber as Neighbor; Schmidt as Smith, and Busjager as Bushacre; while some were entered as John or Fred Dutchman, or Peter Unknown; and one, as Balthus Whiskey, which was rather hard on a German. The tax rolls were equally inaccurate. The 1860 census is nearly as bad, except the fourth assembly district, taken by J. B. Christensen, an educated Dane of Delafield. The 1850 census entered Germans merely as natives of Germany; but that of 1860 generally gives the place of their birth by counties, such as Prussia, Bavaria, or the free city of Bremen. Christensen spells all these countries correctly, while the other census takers mangle them. Bavaria, for instance, is entered as Biron, Bearn and Bern, phonetic imitations of the German Bayern, pronounced "Byern."

Americans reported their employees simply as Germans, knowing nothing about German states and not caring whether they came from Mecklenburg, Alsace or Switzerland. Due allowance should, however, be made for the early officials, for the German characters were like Greek to most of them, while most Germans were then unfamiliar with Latin (English) letters. Then the umlauts, which have no English equivalents, occurring in many names, a modification was necessary whenever written in English. Until the advent of eastern and southern Europeans, German names were the especial stumbling blocks of the Americans. Just imagine them struggling with Schleiermacher, Oestreicher, Henneschid and Hafenberger, which have been Americanized, respectively, to Slaymaker, Austrian, Hendershot and Halfhill. Owing to this difficulty and the natives' prejudice to all things foreign except a French menu, many Germans have followed the lines of least resistance and changed their names.

Thus John Schwarz, who hailed from the same neighborhood in Alsace-Lorraine that my parents came from, translated his name, and as John Black he acquired wealth and political honors in Milwaukee. Sometimes both given and surnames are changed. Thus Rudolph Schmidt changed his name to Rufus Smith, all because his neighbors insisted on calling him that.

Occasionally a name when pronounced phonetically in English as it is spelled, does not appeal to the owner, therefore Rube was turned to Ruby to conform to the German pronunciation. Some names like Nussloch (nuthole), Kuchenbeisser (cake-biter), Ofenloch (stove-hole), Stubenrauch (room-smoke), Schweinefurth (swineford), and Neuneubel (nine-evils), ought to be changed. The last is now pronounced by one of its owners, Noonabell, which is not bad. The name of Knoernschild, proving impossible to many Americans, they simply called a Milwaukee business man "K" until he sensibly capitulated and changed it to Kay. But the Celts will surely claim him should any of his descendants attain distinction. A most curious mutation was the name of Moritz Baisinger, a German Jew, who, when working for an American named Nelson, was called Nelson's Morris, which later evolved into Nelson Morris, the famous Chicago packer who long maintained a summer home on Green Lake.

8. War

Beginning with the Indian outbreak under Black Hawk, the Germans of Wisconsin have proved their loyalty in every war. In the Mexican War, impatient at the delay in local organization, a number of Wisconsin Germans enlisted in an Illinois regiment, among them being Alexander Conze, a brilliant young editor and poet, who fell at Buena Vista. Others took service under the lamented Captain Quarles, these including several commissioned officers, one of whom, Daniel Upmann, succeeded to the command after the former's heroic death. Even Watertown, then a small bustling village, furnished twenty-three German volunteers in that war, so unpopular with free soilers.

Regardless of party, the Germans were intensely loyal to the Union cause in the Civil War, the liberals especially supplying more than their share in men and enthusiastic support. More than 50% of the Turners, all agile, athletic men, took service for the preservation of their adopted country. Twenty-six, or more than one-half the membership of a Manitowoc singing society, enlisted. Says the Waukesha *Democrat* of October 11, 1862: "In the present conflict the Germans have offered freely, and stand among the highest in the ranks of fame." Not only republicans, but such prominent democrats as Dr. Huebschmann, who took service as a surgeon, and editors

Schoeffler of Milwaukee and Rothe of Watertown, spoke in favor of enlistments at German mass meetings. They were commended for their dispatch in organizing, notably in the case of the Ninth Infantry, a regiment wholly German. The Watertown *Democrat* of that period supplies an example of German speed in enlistments. Under date of August 14, 1862, it says:

> Opposite Bertram & Co.'s new store, on Main Street, an immense number of Germans assembled. Theodore Bernhard made a spirit-stirring speech. Flags were flying, torches blazing, drums beating, and all was excitement and activity. The Germans propose to raise an entire company among themselves. Last Tuesday another meeting was held. Lieutenant Kusel assembled the Turner Society.

On August 21st the *Democrat* comments further:

> On Monday the 11th inst., the Germans of this city commenced raising a company for the 20th Wisconsin Regiment. On Friday the 15th, the company was completed – the company numbered 106 volunteers and the next day they took their departure for Madison, and went into camp.
>
> This is a brief story, but speaks volumes for the energy and zeal of our German fellow citizens.

A later edition of the paper reports that the American company, which began recruiting at the same time, did not complete its enlistment till the 28th, and that the Irish had only 28 enlistments. The American company included ten Germans. There were a large number of German commissioned officers in the Wisconsin regiments. In fact they were to be found in nearly every regiment. Many of the German officers and men had seen training in European armies. This training and their innate sense of duty made them good soldiers. In one of the Civil War letters of Private Chauncey H. Cooke, published in the *Wisconsin Magazine of History*, June 1921 , he writes: "I have learned that the Dutch boys make the bravest soldiers. They don't do any bragging and are ready for service no matter how dangerous." The Twenty-sixth, another exclusively German regiment, made a brilliant record in Virginia under Col. William H. Jacobs, and in Sherman's famous march to the sea, under Gen. Frederick W. Winkler. The Twenty-seventh Infantry, preponderantly German, also rendered distinguished service in the southwest under Col Krez. The signal victory at Helena, Ark., shed lustre on

Wisconsin arms, but the victor, Gen. Frederick Salomon, was deprived of his laurels by his superior officer. Says DeLoss Love in *Wisconsin in the War of the Rebellion*, pp. 664-665:

> In Gen. Prentiss' report of the battle, he improperly gives himself credit for the victory, to Gen. Salomon's disadvantage. The brigade commanders, and field staff, and line offices who served in the battle – petitioned President Lincoln for further promotion of Brig. Gen Salomon in view of his merits for this victory. Adjutant Savage, then of the Twenty-eighth Wisconsin, later Colonel of the Thirty-first, wrote Senator T. O. Howe, Aug. 23, 1863, that 'Salomon was in command of all the troops, etc.'

He also writes further that:

> The officers' previous complaints and growling about their heavy fatigue details gave place to expressions of admiration for the prudence, forethought, and admirable management which placed them where they could confidently await the attack of a foe four times their number.

Yet neither Gen. Salomon's official report, nor the petition of the officers was ever published, or came to the hands of President Lincoln. "Jefferson Davis recognized the importance of the battle of Helena by placing it in the list of great disasters which had befallen the Confederate government." Had they won Helena, it would have neutralized Grant's capture of Vicksburg on the same day. General Salomon was, however, later recommended by more generous superior, General Steele, "For gallant and meritorious services at the battle of Jenkin's Ferry," April 30, 1864, where he won a complete victory over a foe four times more numerous. Accordingly he was brevetted Major General. His brother, Gen. Chas. Eberhardt Salomon, was likewise a commander of great ability and bravery. Since the question has been raised, I wish to state that these patriots who rendered such distinguished service to Wisconsin were liberals of Lutheran antecedents. Aside from Major General Carl Schurz, the Germans of Wisconsin furnished Major General Frederick Salomon, and Brigadier Generals Henry Bertram, Conrad Krez, Chas. E. Salomon and Frederick W. Winkler. Edward Salomon, a brother of the generals, succeeded Governor Harvey on the latter's death in April, 1862, and made a splendid executive under the most trying conditions. One instance must suffice. Due to partisan opposition to the draft on constitutional grounds, there was some resistance to its enforcement, resulting in draft riots in New York and elsewhere. But when the draft was resisted at Port Washington, Gov. Salomon quickly suppressed the attempt in striking contrast to the harmful tactics of Gov. Seymour of New York.

In the short Spanish-American War Wisconsin men of German stock were well represented on land and sea.

Although their sympathies may have been largely on the side of the Central Powers at the beginning of the World War, for blood is thicker than water, after our entry into that mighty struggle the German element of the state contributed more than its quota of men and means, as the record shows. Yet, the other so-called foreign stocks, the Irish, Scandinavians, Welsh, English, Scotch, and the more recent arrivals, the Slavs, Italians and Greeks, comprising with German element an overwhelming proportion of our population – all rendered such loyal, tangible support to the American cause that it seems unfair to mention the contributions of one and not the other. However, since thoughtless persons, carried away by their zeal, have cast aspersions upon the loyalty of Americans of German stock, thereby bringing the entire state into disrepute, I may be pardoned for presenting a few facts bearing on the subject.

The case of Walter M. Schatz, of Waukesha, is perhaps typical. Before our country became involved, he used to take sides with Germany against the Allies, but after the declaration of war he was among the first from his country to offer his services, enlisting in the field artillery in Milwaukee in April, 1917, and serving at the front till the end of the war. Yet he was barely eighteen when he enlisted and not subject to draft for nearly a year. The roster of Company L, organized at Waukesha shortly afterward, testified to the same loyalty, for more than 50% of the men were of German descent, although only 42% of the city's population was of that stock. Withal, the declaration came as a shock to many. Less than six months before, President Wilson had been re-elected on the issue that "He Kept Us Out of War," while the republicans protested that they, too, were opposed to it. It is, therefore, not surprising that many, while supporting their country from a stern sense of duty, were sorry that war had come.

This frame of mind was not peculiar to Wisconsin. In an address made in Chicago in the spring of 1918, Samuel Insull, chairman of the Illinois Council of Defense, declared that at the outbreak of the war, 85% of the people of that state were opposed to it, but that through the efforts of their organizations the figures were reversed. It was easy for those who had never liked the Germans and who accepted all the allied propaganda at its face value to be intensely for war and to hate Germany; but to those who had read both sides, or had kindred in the Fatherland, the problem was more difficult. In view of these conditions, and the suspicion unjustly cast upon them, the splendid record of loyalty made by the German element of Wisconsin was not only most laudable, it was heroic. At every turn they heard reflections upon their loyalty, some of the stories being most preposterous. Thus a report was industriously circulated that a prominent citizen of Milwaukee had an arsenal in his cellar to be used in an uprising, and though the lie was officially exploded, his slanderers persisted during the entire war in denouncing him as disloyal. Even religious institutions were subjected to such hateful persecution. The Lutheran seminary at Wauwatosa was searched from cellar to garret for bombs which, it was claimed, were made there and carried out in suitcases by the students. But the zealous sleuths discovered that the suspicious suitcases contained nothing more dangerous than the dirty linen which the students took every Saturday to local laundresses. Those desiring a detailed description of this phase of war hysteria as relates to Milwaukee only, should read, "*The Memories of a Busy Life*," by Gen. Charles King, in the *Wisconsin Magazine of History* for December, 1922. He says in part:

> Hardly had he (Major General Barry) assumed command (at Chicago) when he sent for me to show me reports of dangers ahead in Milwaukee, of German sympathizers who were preparing to resist the registration, burn elevators, armories, manufacturing plants, blow up railway bridges, and play the mischief generally. General Barry knew that I was in close touch with the chief of police and the detective force, and that such things could hardly get a start without our knowing it.

> All the same, there came within a month, sometimes late at night, telephone or telegraphic orders to investigate at once such and such a report of German spies caught red-handed with the tools of their trade in hand, defying the chief of police at West Allis – of threatened uprising among the workmen of our great manufacturing plants. I would investigate and find nothing but darkness and absolute quiet, where there was supposed to be a crowded and seditious meeting.

He continues:

> The local committee of safety, believing that we were sitting on a volcano, besieged the governor and General Barry to mobilize the Second Wisconsin Infantry to protect the city; he tells of a midnight council of leading citizens who implored protection to the American population against seditious bands;

he writes of hordes of secret service men who were also "seein' things," etc. He says, further that even the Secretary of War was being worried by the direful things that might happen, and that finally, when registration arrived, the doom of the city would come. And then he tells how pleased he was to send this dispatch to Gen. Barry: "Registration complete and only disorder from start to finish a fisticuff between two young American citizens, of possible German descent, over the question of which had the right to register first."

Animadversions extended even to the men and women of German extraction in their country's service. When the influenza epidemic was at its worst, reports were persistently circulated, even after official denials, that doctors and nurses of German stock were spreading that dread disease in camps and hospitals! The French were more generous, for in an official order quoted in *Wisconsin's War Record*, page 35, they pay this tribute: "An interesting point is that this division (the Thirty-second) from Wisconsin and Michigan is made up of a great many men of German origin who in thus shedding their blood for the United States gloriously showed their loyalty."

Judging from the casualties among the Wisconsin boys of German stock, they held few dress parade jobs, and thanks to their blood, they were physically fit to fight. The Madison *Capital Times* of April 21, 1919 says on this point:

> Out of a list of 33 boys in Lincoln County who laid down their lives over 20 of them were from fathers and mothers who had come to this country from Germany" (there were 22). "And the story of Lincoln County is the story from all of the so-called German-American sections in the state. The casualty lists for Wisconsin tell the story. Shame on the flamboyant loudmouths who made no real sacrifices themselves and kept up a studied campaign to humiliate and hound and intimidate these people.

As former chairman of the War History Committee of the Waukesha County Council of Defense, I can say that our records confirm the above statement. More than 60% of the Waukesha County boys who met death in action or died of wounds were of recent German descent and one of them was a native of Germany. Robert W. Soat, the first to enlist in Company L, and who died of wounds July 21, 1918, was of this stock, as was Fred Vergens, the first Waukesha County boy to be killed in action.

One of the predominant characteristics of the German immigrants was their strong sense of duty. The late Isaac Stephenson speaks of this in his *Recollections of a Long Life* as follows: Many of those who worked in the lumber camps and at the mills were Germans. They were not very efficient as watermen or for log driving, but steadier than the laborers of any other nationality. Whether or not the watchful eye of the 'boss' was on them, they kept to their tasks with unflagging energy." That this trait is not yet extinct I discovered during the late war.

H. H. Winde, a helpless invalid neighbor of German parentage, who is entirely dependent upon an income barely sufficient for the support of his family, sold securities yielding him 6% and invested the funds in Liberty bonds to the amount of $4,000. Until stopped by my harrowing experiences I undertook, as chairman of the local War History Committee, to interview the nearest kin of Waukesha County's slain to secure their photographs, letters, and a sketch of their lives. When I called on the father of Herbert Lempcke, the grief stricken man spoke feelingly of his faithful son, whom he had expected to relieve him of the management of the farm, concluding with resignation: "But it was our duty to give him to his country. God's will be done."

9. German-American Identity

Lacher included in his work a list of goals and objectives of the Steuben Society of America, no doubt because the Milwaukee unit of the society had published his work. However, they are also of value in providing an overview of where German-Americans stood on a variety of matters and issues, and in conveying what they considered to be the basic elements of German-American identity:

The Steuben Society, founded after World War I, was named in honor of Major General Frederick W. Von Steuben, is a patriotic organization of American citizens of German descent. They indicated the following as their main purposes and objectives:

- Loyalty to our country.

- To study and uphold the basic principles of freedom, tolerance and justice, as established by the founders.

- To protect our country from foreign entanglements, and to preserve it as a sovereign republic – independent politically, economically and culturally.

- To add to the sum total of American achievement by giving wide publicity to the contributions of the German element, and to honor the men and women who have rendered distinguished services to our beloved country.

- To cultivate and preserve the best and noblest qualities of our German heritage – spiritual, social and material – for the enrichment of our descendants in particular and our country in general.

- To protect citizens of German stock from insults, misrepresentation and discrimination.

- To increase self-respect and pride among our descendants that they may become better citizens; to command everywhere due recognition of the contributions and worth of our stock.

IV. Conclusion

Editor's Conclusion

This brief sketch provides an introductory survey of the many dimensions and influences, which can be identified and illuminated with regard to the German element of Wisconsin. Recently, Richard H. Zeitlin has aptly summarized them by observing that "the German imprint on Wisconsin lives on in the names of villages, towns, and streets, in the telephone book of every locality in the state, in the special German ambience of such places as downtown Milwaukee. More subtly, and more importantly, it endures in the commitment to efficient agriculture, to hard work, education, culture, and to the good citizenship and political freedom which were an integral part of the German immigrant's luggage."

It may be said that if anything, Wisconsin is a good example of how Germans and their descendants became German-Americans, thereby giving tangible expression to the advice of Carl Schurz, that one melt the best of the American and the German spirit together in a German-American synthesis.

Selective Bibliography

Sources dealing with the history of Wisconsin's German element can be found in the following list of selective reference and general works:

1. Reference Works:

Arndt, Karl J. R. *The German Language Press of the Americas*. Muenchen: K. G. Saur, 1976-80. A bibliography of German-American newspapers, which is arranged by state, and then by city, or town within the state listings. For Wisconsin's German newspapers, see vol. 1, pp. 647-710.

Hoyt, Dolores and Giles, eds. "Annual Bibliography of German-Americana," *Yearbook of German-American Studies*. For the most recent publications in the field of German-American Studies, see this annual bibliography.

Keresztesi, Michael. *German-American History and Life: A Guide to Information Sources*. Detroit: Gale Research Co., 1980. Regarding Wisconsin, see pp. 95-97.

Merrill, Peter C. *German-American Artists in Early Milwaukee: A Bibliographical Dictionary*. Madison: Max Kade Institute for German-American Studies, University of Wisconsin, 1997.

Pochmann, Henry A., and Arthur R. Schultz. *Bibliography of German Culture in America to 1940*. Millwood, NY: Kraus International Publications, 1982. For references to Wisconsin, consult the subject index.

Pumroy, Eric, and Katja Rampelmann. *Research Guide to the Turner Movement in the United States*. Westport, CT.: Greenwood Press, 1996. Regarding the Turner societies in Wisconsin, see pp. 232-44.

Schultz, Arthur R. *German-American Relations and German Culture in America: A Subject Bibliography, 1941-1980*. Millwood, NY: Kraus International Publications, 1984. With regard to Wisconsin, see vol. 2, pp 948-56.

Tolzmann, Don Heinrich. *Catalog of the German-Americana Collection, University of Cincinnati.* Muenchen: K.G. Saur, 1990. See vol. 1, pp.325-30.

Tolzmann, Don Heinrich. *German-Americana: A Bibliography.* Metuchen, NJ: Scarecrow Press, 1975. See pp. 66-68.

Tolzmann, Don Heinrich. *Upper Midwest German Biographical Index.* Bowie, MD: Heritage Books, Inc., 1993.

2. General Works

Clemens, Lieselotte. *Old Lutheran Emigration From Pomerania to the U.S.A.: History and Motivation, 1839-1843.* Hamburg: The Pomeranian Society, 1976.

Conzen, Kathleen Neils. *Immigrant Milwaukee, 1836-1860: Accommodation and Community in a Frontier City.* Cambridge: Harvard University Press, 1975.

Frank, Louis Frederick. *German-American Pioneers in Wisconsin, 1849-1864.* Translated by Margaret Wolff and edited by Harry H. Anderson. Milwaukee: Milwaukee Historical Society, 1971.

Hale, Frederick. *The Swiss in Wisconsin.* Madison: State Historical Society, 1984.

Hense-Jensen, Wilhelm. *Wisconsin's Deutsch-Amerikaner, bis zum Schluss des neunzehnten Jahrhunderts.* 2 vols. Milwaukee: Die Deutsche Gesellschaft, 1901-02.

Lachner, Bert. *Milwaukee-Wisconsin: Heimat in the Heartland: German-American.* Glen Ellyn, IL: Lachner & Associates, 1995.

Rippley, Lavern J. *The Immigrant Experience in Wisconsin.* (Boston, MA.: Twayne, 1985.

Schelbert, Leo. *New Glarus, 1845-1970: the Making of a Swiss American Town.* Glarus: Komm. Tschudi, 1970.

Tolzmann, Don Heinrich. *German-American Literature.* Metuchen, NJ: Scarecrow Press, 1977. Regarding German-American literature in Wisconsin, see pp. 18-23, 172-78, 196-202, and 291-97.

Wallman, Charles J. *The German Speaking Forty-Eighters: Builders of Watertown, Wisconsin.* Madison: Max Kade Institute for German-American Studies, University of Wisconsin-Madison, 1990.

Zeitlin, Richard H. *Germans in Wisconsin.* Madison: State Historical Society, 1977.

Index

www.ingramcontent.com/pod-product-compliance
Lightning Source LLC
Chambersburg PA
CBHW070517090426
42735CB00012B/2821